The Essential Guide to the Tarot

Take your Tarot studies to the next level with the *Tarot Companion*. It's packed with information about specific card combinations, court card personalities, chakra and color correspondences, and more!

Plus, this book includes a comprehensive dictionary of common symbols found in most Tarot decks. For example, have you ever wondered what that butterfly on the Queen of Swords represents?

Butterfly

The butterfly is a symbol for the astrological sign of Gemini. The butterfly is quick, witty, and versatile and it is no coincidence that the term "social butterfly" was coined to indicate someone who flits around from activity to activity. In Native American teachings, the butterfly represents transformation, which takes on many stages before completion. The egg stage represents a thought or idea. The larva stage indicates that a decision needs to be made. The cocoon stage represents development turning into reality. Lastly, the birth of the butterfly stage indicates that the transformation is complete.

The butterfly, being an airy and mental creature, generally gives us mental processes necessary to help effect change. In esoteric teachings the butterfly represents immortality of the soul because the caterpillar must lie dormant in a cocoon before it emerges from its womb, beautiful and flamboyant. The butterfly is seen in the Minor Arcana on the Knight, Queen, and King of Swords.

About the Author

Tracy Porter is originally from Little Rock, Arkansas, but now lives in England, where she has a career in business. While serving in the U.S. Air Force, she traveled extensively, and earned her B.A. in Computer Studies.

She studies and writes on topics such as numerology, the Tarot, and astrology, is a member of the American Federation of Astrologers, and has been published in a number of British and American magazines, including *Today's Astrologer*, *Prediction Magazine*, and *American Astrologer*. She teaches Tarot classes, and also works as a reader at psychic fairs.

To Write to the Author

If you wish to contact the author or would like more information about this book, please write to the author in care of Llewellyn Worldwide and we will forward your request. Both the author and publisher appreciate hearing from you and learning of your enjoyment of this book and how it has helped you. Llewellyn Worldwide cannot guarantee that every letter written to the author can be answered, but all will be forwarded. Please write to:

Tracy Porter
℅ Llewellyn Worldwide
P.O. Box 64383, Dept. K574-6
St. Paul, MN 55164-0383, U.S.A.

Please enclose a self-addressed stamped envelope for reply, or $1.00 to cover costs. If outside U.S.A., enclose international postal reply coupon

TAROT
COMPANION

AN ESSENTIAL
REFERENCE GUIDE

TRACY PORTER

2000
Llewellyn Publications
St. Paul, Minnesota 55164-0383, U.S.A.

FIRST EDITION
First Printing, 2000

Book design and editing by Connie Hill
Cover design by Lisa Novak
Tarot Cards on cover from *The Sacred Circle Tarot* by Anna Franklin,
    illustrated by Paul Mason

Illustrations from the Rider-Waite Tarot Deck®, known also as the Rider Tarot and the Waite Tarot, reproduced by permisson of U.S. Games Systems, Inc., Stamford, CT 06902 USA. Copyright © 1971 by U.S. Games Systems, Inc. Further reproduction prohibited. The Rider-Waite Tarot Deck® is a registered trademark of U.S. Games Systems, Inc.

Furthermore, the Rider Waite Tarot Deck cannot be printed, published, or produced as a deck of cards.

Library of Congress Cataloging-in-Publication Data (pending)
Porter, Tracy, 1961–
    Tarot companion : an essential reference guide /
Tracy Porter — 1st ed.
    p.   cm.
    Includes bibliographical references and index.
    ISBN 1-56718-574-6
    1. —. 2. —. I. Title.

Llewellyn Worldwide does not participate in, endorse, or have any authority or responsibility concerning private business transactions between our authors and the public.
    All mail addressed to the author is forwarded but the publisher cannot, unless specifically instructed by the author, give out an address or phone number.

Llewellyn Publications
A Division of Llewellyn Worldwide, Ltd.
P.O. Box 64383, Dept. K574-6
St. Paul, MN55164-0383, U.S.A.
www.llewellyn.com

Printed in the United States of America

*Dedicated to
my son, Adrian,
who is always on my mind.*

Contents

Introduction

It is not known exactly where and when the Tarot came into existence, but some believe that it originated in ancient Egypt and was brought to Europe by the Rom, or Gypsies, as they traveled to Europe from India. The oracle's first appearance in Europe seems to have been in the late fourteenth century, probably in Italy, either as a complete seventy-eight-card deck, or as two smaller decks that were later combined to form the version we use today. Because the Tarot was devised using principles of the Cabala, astrology, and numerology, it is possible that philosophers of the day chose to encrypt esoteric secrets into the cards because of religious intolerance. Regardless of how and why the Tarot came into being, it has evolved into a powerful meditative and predictive tool that can help us find answers within ourselves.

How to Use this Book

This book can be used as a reference to help you more fully understand the workings of the Tarot, which has been intricately designed with many subliminal archetypes. While some people are so psychically gifted that they can give a meaningful and accurate reading without a great deal of knowledge of the esoteric arts, the vast majority of us must hone our psychic abilities. In an effort to develop the intuition that is inherent in all of us, a first step in the process is to gain a greater understanding of how the Tarot was designed and why the cards were embellished with particular symbols. Each of the chapters in this book covers the relationship to the Tarot of various disciplines or systems.

An understanding of the symbolism evolving in the cards helps us to gain greater clarity in a reading. The placement of the cards in the spread helps us to understand the circumstances that prompted the reading initially, and how the environment will affect the outcome. Timing is a critical determinant in any reading because we all would like to know when events are likely to occur in our lives.

The elements that are a part of us all are a central theme to the Tarot because each suit is based upon one particular element, helping us to gain a greater understanding of the reading when a predominance of one particular suit appears in that reading. Astrology is a central theme in the development of this oracle because each card in the Major Arcana is associated with a particular planet or sign.

Technologically speaking, we would not be where we are today without the help of a counting system, and for this reason numerology was a fundamental tool that was used to develop the Tarot. Each card was placed in its sequence for a particular reason. Each card has a story to tell, and its placement within the suit shows where we are in the cycle of our evolution. Therefore, the numerical significance of each card is paramount when giving a meaningful reading.

Ten of Pentacles of the Rider-Waite deck shows the Tree of Life trestleboard displayed prominently, thus indicating quite clearly that this science is closely aligned with the knowledge in the Tarot. For this reason, a basic knowledge of the Cabala is essential if we wish to progress from novice to the more advanced stages of reading the Tarot. While the I Ching has evolved separately from the Tarot, it nevertheless can be cross-referenced to the Western disciplines to help us align ourselves harmoniously with worldwide philosophies. The Nordic runes offer us a more grounded approach to our spirituality. We can align each rune to a specific card in the Tarot to give us greater understanding of both oracles.

Chakras, or wheels of energy, are associated with a specific part of the body as well as a color in the spectrum. The scenes depicted on each card in the Tarot are illustrated with various shades of color to add meaning to what is occurring in the background. Therefore, we need a clear understanding of the spiritual interweaving of each color to help us determine nuances that may not otherwise be readily apparent.

Tarot and Synchronicity

The use of the Tarot is based on the *principle of synchronicity*, a term coined by Carl Gustav Jung referring to a meaningful coincidence that occurs without any apparent cause. Any experience that can be attributed to *luck, chance*, or *being at the right place at the right time* is an example of synchronicity. Jung, who asked many religious, esoteric, and spiritual questions while conducting his psychological research, believed that nothing happened just by chance; that there is an underlying principle of the universe relating to this logical reality.

When we use the Tarot we are taking a chance that the resulting spread will reveal some meaningful information that can help us in some way. On a physical level the act of shuffling and drawing the cards is a random act with no relevant meaning to the situation, but on an esoteric level our higher consciousness will intuitively know the positions of the cards within the spread and thus guide the shuffling process so that relevant cards are drawn and laid out in the proper sequence, giving meaning to the reading.

The Tarot as a Problem-Solving and Creativity Tool

The Tarot is a valuable tool that enhances our creativity and problem-solving capabilities. Too often we are not able to see viable alternatives or solutions to problems because we are so enmeshed in the situation we are inquiring about. The simple act of laying out a spread forces us to separate ourselves from distractions and concentrate solely on the object of our inquiry. The Tarot allows us to explore alternatives we may not originally have thought of and shows the circumstance in a way that can reveal aspects of the problem we may have previously overlooked. The Tarot can show hidden agendas and solutions we may not have considered because we have become so deeply involved that we are not able to see the forest for the trees.

Major Arcana

The Major Arcana is thought to have originally been a set of cards separate from the Minor Arcana that was eventually combined with the fifty-six-card deck to make up our present deck of seventy-eight cards.

The Major Arcana is composed of twenty-two cards numbered from 0 to 21. It has direct relevance to the Hebrew Cabala because not only does the number of cards correspond to the number of letters in the Hebrew alphabet, but many of the cards suggest symbolism from the Tree of Life that forms the basis of much of the Cabalistic wisdom. The number of cards in the Major Arcana, twenty-two, is also a master number in the science of numerology.

The Major Arcana depicts the different stages of life we must go through until our soul journey is complete. This journey begins with 0, The Fool, and ends with 21, The Universe. At one time or another we all must go through each stage of the Major Arcana, but we will not necessarily encounter them in sequential order as portrayed by the cards. Through the nature of our existence, we will encounter several beginnings and endings throughout our lifetime that are represented by the archetypes portrayed on the cards.

When performing a reading, the Major Arcana depicts matters relating to the soul, spirit, or destiny of our lives that often indicate karmic themes we must experience. They point out issues that are occurring within our psyche, rather than external everyday events as depicted in the Minor Arcana. Whenever a card of the Major Arcana appears in a spread, special note of that card should be taken because it represents events that will tend to have a profound and lasting impact.

The Minor Arcana

The Minor Arcana is thought to be a separate deck of fifty-six cards that depict the more ordinary details that form a meaningful pattern around our lives. While the Major Arcana tends to portray profound, life-changing events affecting our psyche, most of the cards in the Minor Arcana seem to be less dramatic and portray day-to-day events.

The Minor Arcana consists of fifty-six cards divided into four suits of fourteen cards each. Each suit contains ten numbered cards and four court cards. These suits correlate to the four basic elements of life: fire, earth, air, and water.

1

TRADITIONAL TAROT MEANINGS

While it is not the intention of this work to serve as a "cookbook," those who are just beginning their journey may find that standard interpretations can help give further insight until they have gained sufficient experience and are able to interpret the cards without the aid of reference material. The discussions that follow are accompanied where feasible by the images of the Tarot.

Major Arcana

THE FOOL.

THE MAGICIAN.

0. The Fool

When The Fool appears in your spread, he is urging you to begin a new path. When you are inexperienced you will be protected, and will therefore not encounter too many difficulties along the way. In addition to new beginnings, The Fool may be telling you that you have come upon a crossroad in your life where you must decide which route to take.

1. The Magician

With The Magician, creation is at hand. The Magician is a young person (of any age) who has just completed his training or apprenticeship. He has all of the skills necessary to build upon his future and now needs the opportunity to begin the task of creating something useful. In many ways The Magician can be seen as a young entrepreneur, because he must use his own ingenuity to build his destiny. The Magician is considered to be clever and can amass great wealth through his own devices. Because he is cunning, however, he can be duplicitous when it suits his purposes to do so. For this reason, we all should be wary of this smooth talker until we have learned what lies just beneath his shallow surface that reveals his true soul.

2. The High Priestess

When The High Priestess appears in your spread, she is telling you that you need to look within to find the answers you seek. Many times she indicates disappointment will be coming into your life in some way because you have some lessons to learn about your inner self that can require a rather painful process. When The High Priestess indicates love or romance, it is very unlikely that happiness will come out of the union because she is by association a very independent woman who is not inclined to cater to the whims of male egos.

3. The Empress

When The Empress appears in a spread, fertility, expansion, and abundance prevail. This is an excellent time to begin new projects because they have a high potential for success. In terms of relationships, The Empress brings about happiness, harmony, and sexual fulfillment. She is, however, associated with matriarchal principles, so will at least try to wield her influence over those whom she considers to be a part of her clan.

THE EMPEROR.

4. The Emperor

When The Emperor appears in your spread, you are well on the road to claiming the success you desire. The Emperor often manifests as a powerful person who has the ability to make or break a career.

THE HIEROPHANT

5. The Hierophant

A fitting expression for The Hierophant can be termed "the Sacred Marriage." All relationships started under the influence of The Hierophant are considered very positive and useful liaisons. Sometimes The Hierophant urges you to make a choice about the path you want to take, so a parting of ways could also come about under the influence of this card.

THE LOVERS.

6. The Lovers

When The Lovers appear in your spread, an encounter with someone or something you truly enjoy is forthcoming. If The Lovers appear as a response to a romantic question, a soulmate bond is at hand. When The Lovers appear in response to a creative or business venture, a point of true happiness will be soon coming. It must be emphasized, however, that this soul bond rarely comes without much difficulty, and many weaker foundations will break from the stress. The card depicts three persons, and three people in a relationship is often one person too many.

7. The Chariot

When The Chariot appears in your spread, don't give up because all of the hard work you have invested will soon pay off. The Chariot also often relates to travel, usually in the form of journeys via cars, buses, and trains.

8. Strength

When Strength appears in your cards, you need to maintain an inner strength and resolve. Issues that are forcing you to stabilize your life will soon be coming. You may at times feel under pressure, but rest assured you have within you the ability to handle any difficulties that arise. Strength also indicates that animals will help you through times when you are the most vulnerable.

9. The Hermit

When The Hermit appears in your spread, you may need to spend some time in quiet reflection in order to find the answer to your question. At times The Hermit manifests as a person who gives you sound advice to help you on your path.

10. Wheel of Fortune

When the Wheel of Fortune appears in your spread, your luck is about to change, and ideally for the better. The Wheel of Fortune is generally a positive card that indicates new beginnings, opportunities, and general good luck.

JUSTICE .

11. Justice

When Justice appears, the scales of life will be balanced in some way. If you feel you have been unfairly treated, events will transpire to give you back a little of what you have lost. Sometimes Justice augurs a lawsuit of some kind, but these legalities are necessary to clear the air and restore harmony.

THE HANGED MAN.

12. The Hanged Man

With The Hanged Man, you may feel somewhat at a loss and even have to make a sacrifice of some sort. The Hanged Man indicates that things may be temporarily suspended, which could cause you considerable frustration. The Hanged Man does not mean you won't get what you desire, but it does indicate that you need to have faith and be prepared to wait a while to get it.

13. Death

Death augurs total regeneration and change. When Death appears in a spread, things will never be the same as they were before. Death can be rather paradoxical because sometimes the situation will die a natural death, and other times it will regenerate into something new and beautiful.

14. Temperance

When Temperance appears in a spread, balance and harmony are called for. At times it can be so easy to go overboard in one direction or the other, but what will best ensure a positive outcome is moderation in all aspects.

15. The Devil

When The Devil appears in your spread, it indicates that you are grounded to a certain situation or person by sheer necessity. Under normal circumstances you would not be compelled to pursue the path you are following, but your more earthly instincts are calling you to explore the physical attributes of sex, money, or power. Although you instinctively know your motives and actions are not spiritual in nature, for the time being you must pursue this course.

THE TOWER.

16. The Tower

If you have been living in a glass house, be prepared for someone to throw a few stones. When The Tower appears in your spread, it indicates changes of either a positive or negative nature are likely to transpire that could cause you to reorganize your life plans. You may have your life path in order, but The Tower will place a detour sign along the route so that you must reprioritize.

THE STAR.

17. The Star

The Star is the wish card in the Major Arcana. With The Star, you have many wishes, dreams, and ambitions to which you aspire. It is best to keep your wishes simple so that you can ensure they are met.

18. The Moon

Sometimes The Moon brings about a sense of depression. Circumstances have transpired that cloud your judgment so you are not at this time able to see people or things as they actually are. Insincere persons may be paramount when The Moon appears, so it is therefore wise to keep your own counsel for the time being.

19. The Sun

Where The Moon inhibited your ability to see behind the veils, The Sun seems to lift those sheets so you can see clearly. If you have been uncertain about pursuing a particular course of action, you will soon know what you need to do. The Sun brings with it a lot of brightness and happiness, for illumination has come after a long period of ambiguity.

20. Judgement

Judgement augurs a rebirth, but this regeneration is gentler than that predicted by Death. Judgement serves to heal old wounds that have caused so much pain, and is associated with karma and dharma where we are judged for the life we have led thus far.

21. The World

When The World shows up, you have reached the end of an important cycle in your life. The World indicates union and completion as well as a sense of synergy. With The World, you will soon be encountering a new path to take that will enable you to resume your soul growth.

Minor Arcana—Wands/Rods/Fire

Ace of Wands

The Ace of Wands is the beginning of any creative venture or business pursuit. It indicates optimism and invention, as well as new opportunities and directions.

Two of Wands

The Two of Wands indicates a business partnership of some kind is at hand in which two or more persons will come together to achieve a common goal. It also shows that a balance must be made between attaining worldly possessions and living in poverty.

Three of Wands

The Three of Wands indicates opportunities and success are at hand, but knowledge and skill are essential components if this formula is to achieve rewards.

Four of Wands

The Four of Wands indicates a reunion, quite possibly in the form of a family gathering, will come about that involves building for future prosperity.

Five of Wands

The Five of Wands indicates that events beyond our own control are working at cross-purposes to cause delays, difficulties, and tensions. It may well appear that the persons involved believe they have the situation under control, but forces outside of their sphere of influence are actually calling the shots.

Six of Wands

While many interpretations of this card indicate victory and good fortune, this achievement could be misleading because, although we are on our way, success—the coveted award—has not actually been achieved. Therefore, caution must be exercised because some unexpected events could arise to thwart the anticipated outcome.

Seven of Wands

The Seven of Wands indicates it will be a continuous struggle to stay on top of the situation. We all have obstacles we must encounter on our path to enlightenment and this is one such occasion when we must persevere and keep working in the face of extreme opposition.

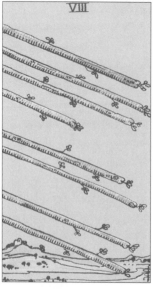

Eight of Wands

The Eight of Wands means travel of a swift nature, as the person involved will be going forward and achieving goals. After much hard work, it seems that things will finally start looking up and accomplishments will be made.

Nine of Wands

The Nine of Wands indicates success after a long struggle to get to the top. There appears to be a bit of weariness because many mistakes have been made and much has been learned the hard way. Additionally, a feeling of defense is in the air because after such a long struggle to achieve success, much vigilance will be necessary to maintain it.

Ten of Wands

The Ten of Wands indicates that a period of hard work lies ahead. While the work involved could be an enormous burden, it is a necessary ingredient to the successes that also lie ahead.

Page/Princess of Wands

The Page or Princess of Wands quite often indicates a young, energetic person will come into the picture to bring a bit of discord.

Knight/Prince of Wands

The Knight or Prince of Wands is a young man who is full of bright ideas, but at present lacks the perseverance to see things through to completion. As a result of this, he will be quite uncertain in his loyalties toward others and should therefore not be trusted until he has matured.

Queen of Wands

The Queen of Wands depicts a woman who has an active and fiery nature. She often represents women in business because she has a good head on her shoulders and is able to make sound decisions.

King of Wands

The King of Wands is an energetic man who is often in a position of leadership—either in business, politics, or religion. He is normally very successful and exudes self-confidence.

Minor Arcana—Pentacles/Disks/Earth

Ace of Pentacles

The Ace of Pentacles indicates a potential for a financial venture. Although the initial seeds of creation are present, proper action must be taken to ensure material gains and prosperity.

Two of Pentacles

The Two of Pentacles indicates that enough money to pay the bills will come just when needed. Tight control of finances is necessary to ensure debt is controlled.

Three of Pentacles

The Three of Pentacles indicates success through skill is at hand. Business will come because of our level of expertise, so it is very important to develop the highest level of competence from the most professional organizations because the quality of experience is very important to achieving success.

Four of Pentacles

The Four of Pentacles means that we should hold on to money and possessions because either the venture is not sound or present wealth will be needed at a later date. Rather than spend, spend, spend—it is far better to save, save, save for that rainy day that will inevitably come.

Five of Pentacles

The Five of Pentacles indicates that the affluent lifestyle we have lived cannot continue. A sense of depression or unhappiness will tend to prevail.

Six of Pentacles

Six of Pentacles is the philanthropic card in the Tarot. Doing good deeds, donating to charity, or embarking on community service are all associated. Additionally, if a favor has been done in the long-distant past, expect it to be returned in some way when least expected and when needed most.

Seven of Pentacles

Seven of Pentacles indicates a time of waiting. All the work has been accomplished and now it needs to develop. This gestation period can often be a difficult one because we wonder if any rewards will be obtained from our efforts.

Eight of Pentacles

With the Eight of Pentacles, we must learn new skills. In this process we are likely to make mistakes before a high level of expertise is achieved. An alternate meaning is that we must set limits on the work we are willing to do. When unscrupulous individuals sense a weakness, they will try to exploit it for their own gain. This tendency is especially prevalent in a depressed economy.

Nine of Pentacles

The influence of the Nine of Pentacles indicates that a plateau of earning has been achieved. This is an opportune time to take a vacation, which will be a well-deserved rest.

Ten of Pentacles

The Ten of Pentacles indicates family money or enterprise. If the querent is self-employed, it is a positive card because this shows he or she will be working for this future and earning money for themself.

Page/Princess of Pentacles

The Page or Princess of Pentacles has two meanings. The first relates to a young person who is earthy and may have a bit of a weight problem. The second indicates the development of a venture or project, which could yield wealth. Special care must be taken to ensure this enterprise progresses smoothly.

Knight/Prince of Pentacles

The Knight or Prince of Pentacles has two meanings. The first indicates a young man who is very practical. The second indicates further development of a material venture which, if handled correctly, could bring about future projects.

Queen of Pentacles

The Queen of Pentacles indicates a pleasant woman who has financial means and money to spend.

King of Pentacles

The King of Pentacles usually indicates a man of financial means. He may not be a business person per se, but has acquired his wealth through an inheritance or legacy of some kind.

Minor Arcana—Swords/Air

Ace of Swords

The Ace of Swords indicates the first initial contact, which is usually by letter writing, telephone calls, or other sorts of correspondence. This card is also associated with the karmic elements of our life, so expect situations that have a ring of destiny to transpire in a most unexpected manner.

Two of Swords

The Two of Swords indicates an argument or parting of ways. The persons involved are not able to find a common point of interest, so the best alternative is to agree to disagree.

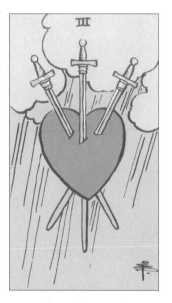

Three of Swords

The Three of Swords indicates heartbreak. This card indicates something, or someone, must be cut out of the querent's life to enable him or her to grow and more fully evolve.

Four of Swords

The Four of Swords is the card of meditation. Nothing must be done for the time being because further guidance will be given later.

Five of Swords

The Five of Swords indicates a verbal argument of sorts. The querent seems to have the upper hand, but it is definitely not a pleasant situation. This is also a card of walking away from a person or situation that is no longer useful in our life.

Six of Swords

The Six of Swords indicates moving away from difficult times. There is a feeling of pain or melancholy associated with this card because much hardship was endured before the decision to move was made.

Seven of Swords

The Seven of Swords is at the best of times a card of superficiality, and at its worst, deceit and slander. When this card appears, we should never expect sincerity or friendship. The best attitude to take is to be courteous and polite, but guard secrets and thoughts diligently because people will tend to either twist words spoken or take credit for other's ideas.

Eight of Swords

The Eight of Swords indicates a type of bondage. This bondage is likely to be verbal in nature as the person in question is not able to say what is on his or her mind. There seems to be a sense of entrapment where the person is not able to move because of prevailing circumstances that are the result of decisions made in the past.

Nine of Swords

The Nine of Swords indicates fear and anxiety as the person in question literally makes himself sick with worry. Sometimes it helps to seek outside assistance to help put the situation into perspective.

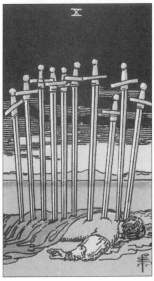

Ten of Swords

The Ten of Swords is the card of ultimate betrayal. This card indicates that hoped-for outcomes are not likely to transpire and a sense of loss will come. When this card is the answer to a question relating to a partnership, it is best to have only minimal dealings with the person referred to because, at best, disappointment is likely to be the outcome of this liaison.

PAGE of SWORDS.

Page/Princess of Swords

The Page or Princess of Swords has two meanings. The first interpretation indicates that a message of some sort is forthcoming. Some communicative development is taking place; care must be taken to ensure it progresses smoothly. The second interpretation of this card is a child or young person who tends to be very chatty.

KNIGHT of SWORDS.

Knight/Prince of Swords

The Knight or Prince of Swords has two meanings. The first interpretation indicates that communication of a more adult nature is coming. The card also represents a young man who is very quick-witted. Care must be taken in dealing with him because if he lacks maturity he can use words to harm others.

Queen of Swords

The Queen of Swords usually indicates a woman who is educated and intelligent, and can be quite a conversationalist when things are going her way. However, negatively she can become bitter and spiteful when she is unhappy with herself.

King of Swords

The King of Swords usually indicates a mature man who is intelligent and well versed. Positively, he can use his intellect and good communication abilities to help others, but negatively he can use his command of language to harm.

Minor Arcana—Cups/Water

Ace of Cups

The Ace of Cups indicates the potential for happiness exists in the situation in question. The soil has been fertilized and now only loving care is needed to bring about fulfillment.

Two of Cups

The Two of Cups indicates happiness and harmony between two people. This could also mean the meeting of two persons, which brings about much happiness.

Three of Cups

Three of Cups indicates happiness and good times in the form of parties, theater, and other types of outings. This is generally a positive and happy card that brings forth lots of fun.

Four of Cups

Four of Cups is doubtful. The person in question is not sure of their feelings and does not feel they will get their heart's desire.

Five of Cups

Five of Cups is a melancholy card. The person in question has been disappointed in some way and is therefore a little depressed. The depression is not as great as that of The Moon, but he or she is nevertheless unhappy. Even through they feel let down, they will be able to learn to help build upon a better future.

Six of Cups

The Six of Cups indicates thinking about the good times from the past. Friends and family may come into the picture, which could bring about recollections of fond memories.

Seven of Cups

The Seven of Cups indicates changes and choices will be forthcoming. There will be several paths to take, but there is no guarantee that the choice made will be the one that will bring about the desired result. Thorough research and analytical thinking needs to be done before making any decisions.

Eight of Cups

The Eight of Cups indicates walking into the unknown. An emotional risk is being taken and one never knows whether it will bear fruit. Another interpretation is to set limits on emotional in-volvement. Sometimes we can put too much emotional energy into relationships or projects, only to be disappointed. It is then that we need to distance ourselves— walk away if necessary.

Nine of Cups

The Nine of Cups is one of happiness and well-being. Many good times and celebrations are likely to occur when this card appears.

Ten of Cups

Ten of Cups is a card of completion as happiness and harmony prevails. It seems as if the ultimate in emotional fulfillment and well-being have been achieved.

PAGE of CUPS.

Knight/Prince of Cups

The Knight or Prince of Cups can have two meanings. The first interpretation is a young man who enjoys life and likes to live it to the fullest. He is generally thoughtful and loving to those he cares about. The second meaning is that a certain emotional situation is progressing nicely.

KNIGHT of CUPS.

Page/Princess of Cups

The Page or Princess of Cups can have two meanings. The first meaning indicates a young child or woman who is sensitive and intuitive. The other interpretation implies that a message will soon be coming. This message may not be blatantly obvious as it could occur from the most unconnected circumstances.

Queen of Cups

The Queen of Cups usually indicates a woman who is sensitive and intuitive. On good days she can be loving and caring, but on bad days rather cranky.

King of Cups

The King of Cups usually refers to an older man who is sensitive and generally acts through his emotions rather than intellect, and who can be extremely jealous at times.

2

THE MAKEUP OF
THE TAROT

Familiarity with the Tarot's structure is key to its reading.

The Suits

The Tarot is composed of four suits that are the forerunners of the suits in a set of playing cards. Each suit corresponds with a particular element that we relate to on a subliminal level, and therefore warrants an in-depth analysis to gain a greater understanding of the deck as a whole.

Wands

The suit of Wands represents the element of fire and the astrological signs of Aries, Leo, and Sagittarius. Fire brings life, love, romance, and creativity into our lives. Cards in the suit of Wands tend to represent enterprise and distinction. There is generally a lot of activity and excitement in this suit by the very nature of its element. Traditionally, Wands represent energy, growth, animation, enterprise, and glory. Because of the creative attributes of this suit, many readers give Wands psychic and spiritual connotations as well.

Pentacles

The suit of Pentacles represents the element of earth and the astrological signs of Taurus, Virgo, and Capricorn. Earth brings practicality, materialism, and a sense of service to our lives. Cards in the suit of Pentacles represent work, accomplishment, and the acquisition of wealth, materials, and possessions. It also governs sensuous pleasures in life, such as good food, drink, and sensual indulgences. Traditionally, Pentacles represents money, material gain, and industry. This suit is totally necessary for a fulfilling spiritual life. Many assert that we must sacrifice our possessions in order to obtain spirituality. If our physical necessities are not taken care of, however, we will as a rule direct our attentions to satisfying those needs before we can even begin to ponder the more meaningful spiritual questions in this life.

Swords

The suit of Swords represents the element of air and the astrological signs of Gemini, Libra, and Aquarius. Air brings mental activity and intellect into our lives. Cards in the suit of Swords tend to depict thinking, communications, messages, and making short trips. Because air is a communicative element it can often lead to arguments, gossip, and strife. Because of its propensity for conflict, the suit of Swords is generally regarded as being unsettled, as there subsequently seem to be latent struggles and animosity present in many of the cards in this suit. Traditionally, Swords represent aggression, force, ambition, courage, strife, and misfortune, but the negative aspects of the cards in the suit can be lessened by maintaining a positive attitude.

Cups

The suit of cups represents the element of water and the astrological signs of Cancer, Scorpio, and Pisces. Water brings pure love, sensitivity, and intuition into our lives. Cards in the suit of Cups tend to depict love, happiness, family, celebration, partnerships, and commitment. This suit also represents intuition, emotion, fantasy, and surrealism. Traditionally, Cups represent love, happiness, emotion, fertility, and beauty.

Court Cards in a Reading

Although court cards in a reading can indicate abstract concepts, they normally represent real people who we will encounter during our day-to-day lives. As previously discussed, if the card in the outcome position of the reading is a court card, it very likely is an indication that the person associated with that card either has the solution or plays an integral part in the successful resolution of the circumstances that prompted the reading.

When a card appears in the outcome position of the layout, it may be necessary to perform another reading concentrating specifically on the card that was pulled. The new reading should reflect how this person will affect the outcome and what role he or she will play.

The Importance of the Fool

The Rider-Waite Tarot Deck is one of the most popular decks in use today. Because the pictures are descriptive and easy to understand, this is the deck many Tarot apprentices begin with on their Tarot journey. Because of its popularity, many newer versions of Tarot are formatted in the same fashion. The Rider-Waite and many of its successors have placed The Fool in position 0, Strength in position 8, and Justice in position 11.

Prior to the production of the Rider-Waite deck there were other versions in use such as the Marseilles version. These decks placed Justice in position 8, Strength in position 11, and the unnumbered Fool between 21, Judgement, and 22, The World.

Dr. Waite, in his process of analysis, placed The Fool at 0, which positioned it at the beginning of the pack. The Fool as an unnumbered card placed between Judgement and The World has much more subtle implications that warrant greater study. After careful reflection its meaning will become apparent to those who sincerely wish to transcend into higher levels of understanding concerning this archetype.

By using the process of analysis, there are actually three places in the Major Arcana where The Fool can be posited: at the beginning before 1, The Magician; after 13, Death; and after 20, Judgement.

When The Fool is placed at the beginning of the Major Arcana it signifies the beginning of a new path. This matter could relate to love, business, money, or any other important area. Sometimes The Fool represents a new beginning, a fresh start in life.

When The Fool is placed after 13, Death, it signifies a major transformation of such magnitude that a new entity has emerged from the ashes. Of course, the new entity is actually the same person, but the change has had so dramatic an effect that for all intents and purposes a rebirth has occurred. What has been can never again be.

When The Fool is placed after 20, Judgement, it signifies that a resurrection has occurred. Judgement and Death are similar in meaning to each other because Death represents a major change in the physical world which could be quite traumatic, while Judgement represents a major change in the spiritual world which is often a little easier for many to cope with. Death can be quite cutting, but Judgement has a smoother approach which is gentler in nature. The new being who has been resurrected by Judgement will be stronger and able to deal with life's events more easily than before. Because he has successfully encountered the tasks called for in the previous twenty cards, he is ready to complete the cycle indicated by 21, The World, and begin a fresh start on a new venture.

Wherever The Fool appears in a reading we should take note. The Fool always indicates new beginnings and choices to be made. Interpreting the stage in the cycle of The Fool requires reflection on the situation in question. Is this an entirely new venture? Is it a rebirth after a major change? Or is it a transformation after much needed healing? Those are important questions that need to be asked when interpreting this card.

3

THE PEOPLE IN
THE TAROT

Occasionally individuals will manifest themselves in a reading, usually in the form of a court card in the Major Arcana. In these instances it is necessary for a reader to use their best intuition regarding the matter to promote an accurate interpretation of events. If the querent knows someone similar to the character described by the card, this is a good indication that it represents an actual person. Even if the querent is not yet aware of such a person, one may come into the picture at a later date to fulfill the reading. If the reader is not sure whether a card depicts a person or circumstance, it is best to inform the querent of all possible aspects relating to the card.

Persons Represented in the Suits

Wands

A court card in the suit of Wands represents a person who is fiery, active, energetic, and lively. He or she is likely to be very involved in getting what they want out of life and most probably they have the astrological signs of Aries, Leo, or

Sagittarius highly placed in their natal horoscope. They will have a lot of energy, drive, and a tremendous will to succeed. They are generally very assertive and can be aggressive in their pursuit of success. They enjoy life, want to have a good time, and can be quite egocentric in the pursuit of their wishes.

Pentacles

A court card in the suit of Pentacles represents a person who is practical, earthy, and grounded. He or she is likely to be involved with work, getting establishing in their career and accumulating wealth. They very likely have the astrological signs of Taurus, Virgo, or Capricorn strongly aspected in their natal horoscopes. They are sensuous and enjoy their earthly pleasures. They generally like to make money, own property, and need to be surrounded by luxury. Because they are primarily concerned with the material and sensual aspects of life, they may have a tendency to overindulge in food, sex, drink, or recreational drugs.

Swords

A court card in the suit of Swords represents a person who is witty, intelligent, and sociable. He or she is likely to be involved with communications, relationships, or socializing on some level. They will most probably have the astrological signs Gemini, Libra, or Aquarius strongly aspected in their birth horoscopes. They are verbal and intellectual, and must be mentally stimulated or will easily become bored. They enjoy socializing and need a varied assortment of friends to accommodate their diverse interests.

Cups

A court card in the suit of Cups represents a person who is warm, emotional, intuitive, and caring. He or she is likely to be highly sensitive, emotional, and psychic. They very likely have the astrological signs of Cancer, Scorpio, or Pisces strongly aspected in their birth horoscope. They are very sensitive and caring, and this sensitivity can range from pure to compulsive love. Because they have such high ideals they may fantasize too much or become depressed when reality doesn't meet their expectations.

The Court Cards Found in the Suits

The King normally represents an older or mature man. The Queen normally represents an older or mature woman. The Knight or Prince normally represents a young man. The Page or Princess normally represents a young woman or child.

Persons Represented in the Major Arcana

People can sometimes manifest themselves as characters in the script of the Major Arcana. Usually, when a card in the Major Arcana represents a person, he or she is likely to have a profound impact on the person's life.

The Fool

As a person, The Fool represents someone who is just starting out in pursuit of a path. This person is usually inexperienced in what he or she is doing and will have to learn the skills necessary to ensure success. Many times The Fool is actually the querent in the reading.

The Magician

As a person, The Magician is someone who has just completed his or her training and now needs to go out and create their own destiny based upon what they have learned. They are also somewhat smooth talkers, and things do not appear as they seem. Therefore, caution must be exercised when dealing with this person because he or she may be an adept confidence artist.

The High Priestess

As a person, The High Priestess is an independent woman who can carry with her a lot of emotional scars that are the reason she is not able to form harmonious relationships with others. Actually, her independence is merely a facade, because in reality she yearns for closeness, but fears rejection. Because The High Priestess has been hurt by those she trusted, she has learned to rely on herself instead of placing her self-worth into the hands of others.

The Empress

As a person, The Empress is an older woman who may be the matriarch of the family. She has power merely because she gave birth to her family clan. If she is of a jealous disposition she can wreak havoc on the lives of outsiders who seek to come into the family unit.

The Emperor

As a person, The Emperor is a powerful man. Even if he is not the designated boss, he nevertheless has the power to influence a person's career or destiny.

The Hierophant

As a person, The Hierophant is usually a religious person or teacher who possesses much wisdom and knowledge.

The Lovers

As persons, The Lovers are a couple in love. Because both persons in this union are in the first stages of courtship, they do not yet realize the other is not a perfect human being. There is also someone who can be seen as an intruder into a relationship and much skill will be necessary to effectively deal with him or her.

The Chariot

As a person, The Chariot is someone who is always on the move. He or she will ultimately find success because he is persistent and will never accept defeat.

Strength

As a person, Strength is often a strong-willed individual who is usually in a position of leadership. These people are often not the official leaders, but have been elected by their peers as the group's unofficial leader because of their level-headedness and good judgment. Often this person has had to encounter many trials, which gives him or her the wisdom to make sound decisions. Strength can manifest as a person who enjoys the company of animals.

The Hermit

As a person, The Hermit is somewhat of a loner who is more comfortable in his own company. Many times The Hermit manifests as the querent in the reading because all of the answers he seeks are actually within.

Wheel of Fortune

As a person, the Wheel of Fortune is someone who the querent was destined to meet in order to bring about life-changing events.

Justice

As a person, Justice is a rational, logical person who generally acts as a mediator. He or she does not let emotional ties get in the way of their judgments and therefore don't lose any sleep if anyone is unhappy with the decision they have made.

The Hanged Man

As a person, The Hanged Man is somewhat of a martyr who tends to live life based on faith rather than taking control of his or her own destiny.

Death

As a person, Death is someone who brings about profound and extreme changes.

Temperance

As a person, Temperance takes life easy and doesn't do anything in extremes because his or her ultimate goal is equilibrium.

The Devil

As a person, The Devil is someone who is involved with earthly pursuits. He or she may not necessarily be a friend, but the querent must work with this person in some way before they can progress unto other levels of reality.

The Tower

As a person, The Tower is someone who shakes things up a bit. He or she often causes a lot of animosity because people don't generally like change, which must inevitably transpire if we are to evolve.

The Star

As a person, The Star is someone who brings hope to the querent.

The Moon

As a person, The Moon is very illusive. At times The Moon can be insincere, so the querent must watch carefully for any deceit.

The Sun

As a person, The Sun is happy and cheerful. He or she brings along a lot of illumination and can be a breath of fresh air to the weary. The Sun, however, can at times be arrogant and may consider him- or herself to be superior in some way to the querent.

Judgement

As a person, Judgement is usually someone with whom the querent has had dealings in a past life and they have agreed to meet up with again in this life to settle some unfinished business. Judgement can be positive or negative, but his or her influence depends mainly on what has transpired ages ago.

The World

As a person, The World brings with him or her the final events to a scenario that has reached its conclusion. After meeting the person represented by The World, the querent will need to begin a new path because the situation has been resolved.

4

COMBINATIONS
IN SPREADS

The Tarot is a subtle tool that speaks to us in many different ways. In addition to the outcome position, which is implied at the end of many layouts, the Tarot also often presents hidden agendas by including messages that can be deciphered by looking at the combination of numbered cards in the spread. The number of cards has specific indicators of how they relate to the situation.

One Card in a Reading

One numbered card in a reading reflects that particular element is central and concerns the querent and his or her sole surroundings.

Two Cards in a Reading

When two cards of a common number or court appear in a spread, this indicates that two people or circumstances are likely to be involved in the outcome. This generally refers to two people getting together to form a union or partnership of some kind.

Three Cards in a Reading

When three cards of a particular number or court appear in a reading, a group of three or more people is likely to get together and discuss the subject. The outcome of this discussion is likely to have an impact on the outcome of the situation.

Four Cards in a Reading

When four cards of a number or court appear in a spread, a solid foundation is going to be established. The solidity of the four tends to ground the situation to give it stability so that the outcome is almost certain. The number four is also a number of hard work, so much labor is likely to come to the querent when four cards appear.

Aces in a Reading

Four Aces

Four Aces in a reading signify an important time ahead. Much happiness is possible, but a wrong move can lead to danger. This is a time to tread carefully and make sure any decisions made are not irrevocable.

Three Aces

Three Aces in a reading signify a positive placement indicating that good news is forthcoming. Three people or important elements will come into being that are vital to the successful completion of the scenario.

Two Aces

Two Aces in a reading indicate a union or partnership of some sort is likely to occur. If the Ace of Cups and the Ace of Pentacles fall together, this union has the potential to bring much material happiness.

Twos in a Reading

Four Twos

Four twos in a reading indicate groups of people working together for the common good. These groups can be either professional or social in nature.

Three Twos

Three twos in a reading indicate there are likely to be reassessments, reshuffling, or rescheduling.

Threes in a Reading

Four Threes

Four threes in a reading herald a time of creativity and productivity. Several people are possibly working together to complete a project.

Three Threes

Three threes in a reading often warn of lies and deceit. People may be involved in gossip and things may not be exactly as they appear.

Fours in a Reading

Four Fours

This placement reveals security, contentment, and a welcome rest. Financial security through work and sound investments are indicated.

Three Fours

Three fours indicate much work is necessary to bring about successful completion of the project at hand.

Fives in a Reading

Four Fives

Competitive influences are indicative of this placement. Any partnerships formed are likely to be unstable and ultimately unfulfilling. It may transpire that the participants are actually competitors working at cross-purposes to each other.

Three Fives

A solid routine and regular cycles are necessary to positively influence the situation.

Sixes in a Reading

Four Sixes

Four sixes indicate balance and harmony. If relationships have been difficult, they should soon improve.

Three Sixes

Three sixes indicate completion of a project or cycle. A goal has been achieved and there is reason for celebration.

Sevens in a Reading

Four Sevens
Because of the illusionary influences surrounding this mysterious number, pitfalls and disappointments are likely to occur.

Three Sevens
Three sevens harbor a happy result to a situation that at first seemed doubtful.

Two Sevens
Two sevens show a balance of forces with mutual love and harmony. This situation is likely to involve two people and some spiritual ideals are likely to have been met.

Eights in a Reading

Four Eights
Because the number eight typically implies work and responsibilities, four eights herald a time of much activity and news surrounding the type of work one does.

Three Eights
Three eights indicate news of an important alliance is at hand. This alliance will likely advance the stature of those involved and could even indicate a marriage or partnership of some kind.

Two Eights
Surprise developments are likely to occur when two eights appear in a spread.

Nines in a Reading

Four Nines

Four nines in a reading represent accomplishment. There is much to be happy about because an important goal has been achieved.

Three Nines

Three nines typically represent the attainment of the three primary areas we are generally concerned with: health, wealth, and happiness.

Two Nines

Important news or documents will be arriving soon, which relate to business matters.

Tens in a Reading

Four Tens

Four tens depict an overwhelming success that has been obtained through sometimes overwhelming stress and tension. Sometimes there will be obstacles to overcome before success is finally achieved.

Three Tens

There is likely to be some legal matter that needs to be resolved. There is also the possibility of business correspondence that will soon arrive to help resolve the issue.

Two Tens

Two tens in a reading indicate new jobs, duties, or responsibilities. Lucky breaks concerning the question are not uncommon.

Pages in a Reading

Four Pages

Four pages in a reading symbolize groups of young people or students congregating together. These gatherings could be at schools, universities, and other places where young people can be found.

Three Pages

There are likely to be a lot of pleasant gatherings and social activities concerning young people.

Two Pages

Two pages signify two young people getting together. There is the possibility of gossip or other trouble associated with friendships.

Knights in a Reading

Four Knights

Four knights in a reading indicate that there is much male energy present in the situation. There may be a group of young men who actively influence the outcome.

Three Knights

Three knights in a reading indicate gatherings are possible. These parties are likely to be more *adult* in nature than the occasions depicted by the pages.

Two Knights

Two knights indicate a meeting of old friends.

Queens in a Reading

Four Queens

When four queens appear in a spread, a group of people is likely to gather for some form of entertainment. Because of the feminine nature of the queen, the group will generally consist primarily of women.

Three Queens

When three queens appear in a spread, a group of women are likely to gather together over refreshments, which may be a tea, coffee, or luncheon. The ladies will offer moral support or advice to help resolve any dilemmas.

Two Queens

When two queens are in a reading, there is likely to be gossip, secrets, rivalry, or jealousy.

Kings in a Reading

Four Kings

Four kings in a spread denote very powerful gatherings of a professional nature.

Three Kings

Three kings in a spread indicate groups of powerful, influential men forming social gatherings. These groups could consist of leisure or professional clubs.

Two Kings

Two kings in a spread indicate a business partnership or enterprise is at hand.

5

TIMING AND
THE TAROT

The Tarot can be used to time certain events in life that may occur when certain cards in the Minor Arcana appear before or after a card from the Major Arcana.

If card numbers 2, 3, 7, or 9 appear immediately before or after a card from the Major Arcana, a conjunction occurs. This conjunction should be interpreted separately from the initial reading because it adds an additional *layer* to the reading and gives greater clarity to the querent's circumstances. If more than one conjunction appears in a spread, these two configurations should be interpreted separately, because in all probability they refer to separate events.

The Minor Conjunction

If a number 2, 3, 7, or 9 card from the Minor Arcana appears immediately before a card from the Major Arcana, a minor conjunction occurs that indicates that the querent is beginning to embark on a new cycle. The energies inherent in this cycle are determined by the energies specified in the cards.

Twos

The number two generally refers to challenges in partnerships, which almost always refer to couples, partnerships, duality, and pairs. Two as one more than one refers to our need to extend our level of awareness beyond our egocentric concerns to those of our partner or friend.

Two of Wands = Two Days

An event is likely to occur within two days that may concern business partnerships or creative endeavors. The nature of the beginning cycle will be indicated by the Major Arcana card, which follows the Two of Wands. Because the suit of Wands is so active, the cycle should begin shortly after the reading.

Two of Cups = Two Weeks

An event is likely to occur within two weeks that concerns relationships involving attachments of a highly emotional nature.

Two of Swords = Four Weeks

An event is likely to occur within four weeks concerning communications with a friend or partner. Contracts, phone calls, and other forms of communication will figure prominently.

Two of Pentacles = Two Months

An event is likely to occur within two months. During this period, the querent needs to focus on property, money, and financial matters. These financial concerns may be the result of an agreement with another person.

Threes

Threes refer to expansion and growth, and signify a need for independence because they are one more than the coupling two.

Three of Wands = Three Days

In approximately three days the querent will receive further guidance concerning issues relating to the card depicted in the Major Arcana. These concerns will deal with a creative endeavor or business pursuit.

Three of Cups = Three Weeks

In approximately three weeks the querent will find that a part of his or her destiny is coming into effect, which could represent the beginning, continuation, or change of plans. This could be a very emotional time with expectations of much happiness. The card drawn from the Major Arcana will give further clues to the situation.

Three of Swords = Six Weeks

During the upcoming six-week period the querent is likely to feel a sense of loss. Although he or she may feel a bit melancholy, the worst of this difficult time will be over soon with the resulting outcome reflected in the card from the Major Arcana.

Three of Pentacles = Three Months

During the upcoming three-month period the querent will be preparing for awards and recognition. Success is likely, but he or she will need to persevere and develop their skills in order to assure a positive outcome. The Major Arcana card following the Three of Pentacles will show the querent the area in which they will achieve.

Sevens

When a seven precedes a Major Arcana card, a choice needs to be made. The querent has reached a crossroad in her or his life and must make a choice before continuing on their journey. The seven deviates from the general pattern of the previous conjunctive cards because each suit of seven will be activated in approximately seven days.

Seven of Wands = Seven Days

The upcoming week may be rather tense for the querent as his or her concerns center on business or creative matters. They may be required to stand up for themselves or defend their area of expertise. The following Major Arcana card will reflect the nature of this situation.

Seven of Cups = Seven Days

In the upcoming week the querent needs to expand his or her level of awareness and look closely at the opportunities available to them, because some of the alternatives may not deliver hoped-for outcomes. Although things may not be readily apparent, the querent will soon begin to see with greater clarity.

Seven of Swords = Seven Days

During the upcoming week, the querent needs to reevaluate his or her current situation. They may have been influenced by a proposition that seemed too good to be true; they will realize that they have been deceived. Because of this, they may be inclined toward self-pity, but instead should concentrate their efforts on future prospects provided by the card drawn from the Major Arcana.

Seven of Pentacles = Seven Days

During the upcoming week, the querent needs to arrive at a decision regarding his or her career, possessions, or finances. It seems that they have put in a great deal of effort and are now entering into a period of gestation. It is important to know that if this preparation was of a solid foundation, the outcome will be stable, but if the querent failed to properly prepare, then the outcome may not be what they desire. Nevertheless, the situation will come to fruition during the upcoming week and the associated card pulled from the Major Arcana will indicate the nature of the outcome.

Nines

Nine represents the end of a cycle in traditional numerology and is considered one before the end in the Tarot, with the ten representing completion. Nines generally have a lot of power, which is cultivated through the previous eight cards. With nine, the querent feels the need to go back and reflect, reevaluate, and release that which he or she no longer needs. Each nine is stimulated in two stages comprised of twenty-eight days. The first stage is composed of nine days and all existing forces will be broken down during this period. The second stage lasts for a duration of nineteen days and during this period the new cycle begins.

Nine of Wands = Nine Days Followed by Nineteen Days = 28 Days

During this period, the querent needs to finish what he or she has started. It is not the time to give up because with a little extra effort they can reach their goal. The associated card from the Major Arcana reflects what they are likely to encounter during this new cycle.

Nine of Cups = Nine Days Followed by Nineteen Days = 28 Days

During this period, the querent is likely to experience a lot of joy and happiness. He or she should experience their first element of joy within the first nine days, and the remaining days will strengthen the initial peak.

Nine of Swords = Nine Days Followed by Nineteen Days = 28 Days

During this time, the querent will find that he or she is letting go of a lot unpleasant thoughts. They may be reluctant to release these opinions that have been with them for such a long time, but in order for them to enter into the next cycle it is important to let go of these memories.

Nine of Pentacles = Nine Days Followed by Nineteen Days = 28 Days

During this time the querent is likely to experience significant events relating to money or material possessions. He or she may feel that their life is at an impasse because nothing is right, yet nothing is wrong either.

Major Conjunctions

A major conjunction occurs when a card from the Major Arcana appears before a timing card. This indicates that the major event has already appeared in the querent's life, and the influences of the card impact the native first, as she or he then experiences the energies represented by the Minor Arcana timing card to complete the conjunction. The difference between these two types of conjunctions is that the major conjunction signifies the end of a cycle, while the minor conjunction depicts the beginning of one.

6

THE SYMBOLISM OF
THE TAROT

Most Tarot decks available today are remarkably similar, except for a few minor variations that appear on some of the cards. The reason Tarot takes a parallel line of reasoning from one Tarot master to another is because a universally understood esoteric system of symbolism was used to produce the symbols on the cards. Each card has been intricately designed and drawn to include its true meaning through the use of symbols, which are universally acknowledged through our unconscious minds. These symbols, when fully understood, will give the Tarot reader the necessary tools to perform an insightful reading merely by studying the depictions on each card.

Of course, after several years of careful reflection of this oracle, each card will begin to develop its own meaning for each person. After each picture has been studied and thoroughly understood, it is only necessary to think of the card to obtain a clear understanding of the situation at hand.

As you progress in your understanding of the esoteric symbolism of the Tarot, you will likely begin to use your intuition more when interpreting the cards. These feelings you get will eventually help you gain greater inner knowledge of the esoteric meaning of each card.

The Tarot has traditionally been considered to be of Western European origin, so themes associated with this culture will generally prevail in the cards. Other cultures, such as the Japanese and Native American, have become familiar with this type of divinatory tool and have consequently developed their own decks that reflect themes particular to their own cultural awareness.

The descriptions that follow relate to the Rider-Waite and similar decks.

Angel

The angel is a symbol of the superconscious. A messenger who is many times unaware of the role he or she plays in imparting news or information. Each of us is said to have at least one guardian angel that we can contact through meditation. Our guardian angels watch over us, and only have our best interests at heart. Angels are seen in the Major Arcana on 6, The Lovers; 14, Temperance; and 20, Judgement.

Ankh

The ankh is the Egyptian symbol of eternal life, truth, and regeneration. Because of the ankh's resemblance to the glyph for the planet Venus, many people equate this symbol with love and beauty. The ankh is also called "the mirror of Venus." The ankh is seen in the Major Arcana on 4, The Emperor.

Anubis

Anubis is a jackal-headed Egyptian god who represents the evolution from lower to higher levels of consciousness. He is the Egyptian equivalent of Mercury, and therefore represents intellect, communication, teaching, writing, and the relaying of messages. Anubis is seen in the Major Arcana on 10, Wheel of Fortune.

Banner

The banner represents freedom from the material realms. The banner carried in the left hand indicates that the level of awareness has passed from the conscious self to the subconscious self, and has become automatic. The banner is seen in the Major Arcana on 10, Wheel of Fortune; 13, Death; 19, The Sun; and 20, Judgement.

Bed

The bed is considered to be a vehicle of rest, relaxation, and even pleasure. The purpose of the bed provides a clue as to the nature of the situation. For instance, a bed in a hospital will have completely different implications than a bed in a hotel room. A bed can be seen in the 9 of Swords and the 4 of Swords.

Boat

A boat is seen as a medium to get us from one point to another—quite often through a sea of emotions. If the boat is of good construction then we will receive a great deal of support. If, on the other hand, it is tiny or not well built, then it will be unlikely that we will receive assistance in our endeavors. A boat can be seen on the 6 of Swords and the 2 of Pentacles.

Book

Books contain knowledge that must be assimilated before further illumination can be achieved. Books are, however, very subjective devices that reveal the inherent motives of their authors. Therefore, a close look at the credibility and authority of the creator of each work will be necessary in order to determine the validity of the contents of that work.

Bull

The bull, symbol of the astrological sign Taurus, also represents the earth element, and is assigned to the suit of pentacles. It is stable, reliable, enduring, and sensual. The bull is extremely patient and steadfast when working on attaining a goal for himself. The bull appears on 10, Wheel of Fortune; and 21, The World.

Butterfly

The butterfly is a symbol for the astrological sign of Gemini. The butterfly is quick, witty, and versatile, and it is no coincidence that the term "social butterfly" was coined to indicate someone who flits around from activity to activity. In Native American teachings, the butterfly represents transformation, which takes on many stages before completion. The egg stage represents a thought or idea. The larva stage indicates that a decision needs to be made. The cocoon stage represents development turning into reality. Lastly, the birth of the butterfly stage indicates that the transformation is complete. The butterfly, being an airy and mental creature, generally gives us mental processes necessary to help effect change. In esoteric teachings the butterfly represents immortality of the soul, because the caterpillar must lie dormant in a cocoon before it emerges from its womb, beautiful and flamboyant. The butterfly is seen in the Minor Arcana on the Knight, Queen, and King of Swords.

Cabala

The Cabala is a system of Jewish mystical thought that attempts to put the essence of events that occur in the universe into clear perspective. The Cabala can be seen on the 10 of Pentacles.

Cat

Cats are intuitive, instinctive, aloof, detached, psychic, and sexy. Sometimes they are uncaring, sneaky, relaxed, uncooperative, and playful. They often symbolize hidden fears or loving memories. The black cat represents the more negative aspects of the planet Venus and is pictured on the Queen of Wands.

Chain

Chains are self-imposed restrictions. Chains can, on some level of reality, represent security because they impose limits and boundaries that we dare not trespass. Chains also represent dependence because it is often easier to stay in a bad situation due to obligations rather than pursue the unknown in search of freedom. Chains are seen on 15, The Devil.

Chair

Chairs generally represent a support mechanism, which is essential in order to achieve success. The chair will generally be more opulent with the increased status of the person using it. A chair can be seen on 4, The Emperor; and 3, The Empress.

Circle

A circle is actually a polygon with an infinite number of sides, representing eternity, spirit, completeness. The circle is a symbol of God, perfection, unending love, and the super-conscious. The circle is seen on 10, Wheel of Fortune; and 21, The World.

Coffin

A coffin is considered to be a receptacle to hold things that are waiting to be reborn into another sphere of existence. A coffin also represents a loss in one form or another, but with this emptiness will come new opportunities and success. A coffin can be seen on 20, Judgement.

Clouds

Clouds represent a psychic veil that must be transcended. There are many emotions that have been kept at bay, but which must soon be revealed. If the clouds are bright it indicates a feeling of upliftment and spirituality, but if dull, depression is imminent. Clouds can be seen on 10, Wheel of Fortune; 21, The World; and 16, The Tower.

Crescent

The crescent represents the soul. The crescent is seen on 2, The High Priestess.

Cross

The cross is an ancient symbol that predates Christianity. It represents humanity's incarnation on earth, its death and regeneration. The solar cross indicates the union of masculine and feminine elements. The cross is seen in the Major Arcana on 2, The High Priestess; and 20, Judgement.

Crown

The crown represents the crown chakra. The crown chakra is represented by the color white and is considered to be a direct link to God or the higher self. The crown depicts being master over the self in terms of expanded awareness and spirituality. The crown is seen in the Major Arcana on 3, The Empress; 5, The Hierophant; and 16, The Tower.

Cube

The cube is sometimes depicted as a square. The square represents earth, material matters, and earthly concerns. The square has four sides and the number four is very significant to practicality, reliability, responsibility, and work. It helps us to build our foundations on the earth plane. The cube is seen in the Major Arcana on 15, The Devil.

Cups

Cups are associated with the element of water and are very receptive. Cups represent the astrological signs of Cancer,

Scorpio, and Pisces. Cups are emotional, and this feeling can span from the Cancerian pure, trusting love, to the Scorpionic intense, transforming love, and finally to the Piscean idealistic, sacrificial love. When looking at the cup, it is important to look at its environment and position. Is it upright or overturned? Is it full or empty? What is in the cup? Cups are represented in the suit of Cups, and seen in the Major Arcana in 14, Temperance.

Cypress Tree

The cypress tree is sacred to Venus. Trees often represent the "Tree of Knowledge" and the fruits of our labors. Trees also symbolize new growth and stages of life and death. In Native American teachings, trees are ancient beings that possess much wisdom and contain a great deal of energy that humans can tap into just by being near those majestic beings. The cypress tree is seen in the court cards of the suit of Swords and 3, The Empress.

Devil

The devil represents the base materialistic urges that we feel compelled to satisfy. He is responsible for lust, greed, and sensual pleasures, and is considered to be separate from our spiritual awareness. Many people see the devil as the negative aspects of ourselves, including hate, discord, greed, fear, jealousy, falseness, and destruction. The devil doesn't necessarily have to be evil, but we should try to balance our earthly and sensual desires with a healthy dose of spirituality when the devil appears in our lives. The devil is seen in the Major Arcana in 15, The Devil.

Dog

Dogs are friends, helpers, and companions to humankind. Dogs love unconditionally and are totally loyal to their masters. It is not in a dog's nature to be mean or vicious, but some lose their compassionate natures from abuse, trauma, or a sort of perverse loyalty to their masters. Because dogs are so adoring, humans could learn a few lessons about love and compassion from these selfless creatures. Dogs are the servants of humanity, and people with a strong sense of *dogness* will often be found working as philanthropists, nurses, counselors, ministers, or soldiers. Dogs are also guardians of the world we live in. Throughout history, dogs have guarded hell, the ancient secrets, hidden treasures, and babies while mothers were out working in the fields. The symbol of the dog also indicates that all nonhuman forms of life are elevated and improved by the evolving advancement in human consciousness. The dog is seen in the Major Arcana on 0, The Fool; and 18, The Moon.

Dove

The dove has historically been a symbol of peace and is associated with the astrological sign of Scorpio where the emotional-sexual power is transformed into the healing grace of the dove. In occult teachings the dove is also associated with the group spirit, which is made up of humans who have purified their desire natures to a degree that allows them to experience transpersonal unity in the form of empathy and rapport. In Christianity, the dove is a symbol of peace attained through the arbitrating and healing presence of the Holy Spirit.

Eagle

The eagle is associated with the astrological sign of Scorpio. Where the Scorpion is used to denote the lesser-evolved Scorpio who stings anything or anyone who crosses his path, the eagle represents the more highly evolved Scorpio who has transcended his tribulations and flies high into the sky like the mythological phoenix rising out of its ashes. In Native American teachings, the eagle is a spiritual being who has the ability to live in the realm of spirit while remaining connected and balanced within the Earth realm. The eagle represents a state of grace achieved through hard work, understanding, and a completion of the tests required to achieve personal power. Eagle feathers are sacred to the Native Americans and are used for healing and ceremonies. The eagle is seen in the Major Arcana on 10, Wheel of Fortune; and 21, The World.

Ellipse

The ellipse is the symbol of the superconscious. The ellipse is seen in the Major Arcana on card 21, The World.

Figure 8 on Its Side (Epsilon)

In electronics and mathematics, this is the symbol for infinity and is used primarily when measuring resistance. In esoteric studies this figure symbolizes eternal life, harmonious interaction between the subconscious and conscious, life and feeling, and desire and emotion. This symbol may also mean dominion over the material realms. The figure 8 on its side is seen in the Major Arcana on 1, The Magician; and 8, Strength.

Fish

The fish symbolizes the astrological sign of Pisces, considered to be the most spiritual of the twelve signs of the zodiac. This sign symbolizes emotion, compassion, empathy, psychic impulses and brotherly love. Due to the precession of the equinox, about 2,000 years ago the earth left the age of warring, aggressive Aries, and moved into the sacrificial age of Pisces. Christians have historically used the fish to symbolize their religious beliefs and followings. At about the same time the precession of the equinox was causing the earth to change signs, a man called Jesus of Nazareth walked the earth. Based on astrological and biblical evidence, Don "Moby Dick" Jacobs, a Methodist minister and Bible scholar as well as astrologer, has been able to rectify Jesus the Christ's birthday and time as March 1, 7 B.C. at 1:30 A.M. in Bethlehem. This date would make Jesus a Pisces and not a Capricorn, as has been traditionally assumed to be his sign of birth to coincide with pre-Christian ceremonies of the winter solstice. Therefore, it would have been only fitting to use the symbol of the Piscean fish to represent their belief in Christ in lieu of the goat. Incidentally, the Capricornian goat is actually an animal that has the upper body of a goat and the lower anatomy of a fish. Although well hidden, Capricorn can display the emotional depth and sensitivity of the fish, but it is generally well grounded by the serious and earthly influence of the goat, which tends to maintain dominance. The fish is seen on the Page of Cups card.

Fixed Signs

The fixed signs are depicted on the Wheel of Fortune and The World in the Major Arcana. They are the four fixed zodiacal signs of Taurus (depicted as the bull), Leo (depicted as the lion), Scorpio (as represented by the Eagle), and Aquarius (as represented by the man). These four signs all possess the fixed quality and are composed of the four elements of fire, earth, air, and water, thus bringing much needed stability to an unpredictable world.

Flame or Fire

The flame is the symbol of awareness, light, enlightenment, warmth, and desire. It represents the spirit of God, which can be magical, enlightening, stimulating, transforming, or even destructive. Fire represents passion, enthusiasm, and spontaneity. The Native Americans consider fire to be sacred. There are basically six forms of fire that manifest themselves in many ways. One primary source of fire relevant to esoteric studies is the flame within us called the solar plexus. It is the life force within us that keeps us alive and healthy. When we shut parts of ourselves off from the world, these centers become cold. After time, this imbalance turns to disease, so it is therefore essential that our entire beings are filled with the flame of life. Flames can be seen on 16, The Tower.

Flowers

Flowers depict spiritual thoughts, love, and happiness. They represent kindness, caring, joy, compassion, and grace. Flowers are an expression of love, beauty, freedom, and healing qualities. Flowers are seen on the 6 of Cups.

Fruit

Fruit represents fertility. It implies the results of what we have planted.

Gnomes

Gnomes are ageless dwarves who live beneath the surface of the earth. They are said to guard precious metals and treasures. Gnomes are associated with the suit of Pentacles because they are so close to the earth.

Goat

In earlier times, the goat was associated with the more evolved members of the human race who were responsible for imparting the impulses that guide and inspire human culture throughout the centuries. The goat is the symbol for the astrological sign of Capricorn, which is serious, responsible, and materialistic. Because the goat is so close to earthly concerns, it can easily succumb to its most basal desires, which may be seen as the vices of lust, greed, envy, and avarice. In the Major Arcana, the goat on 15, The Devil has succumbed to such lusts. The goat is also seen as a fertility symbol, and is shown in the arms of the Queen of Pentacles.

Gold

Gold is the metal that represents the Sun. Gold is the color of the solar plexus, and the life force emanates from that chakra located just above the navel in the body. On the mental or emotional level, the solar plexus represents power issues, control issues, accomplishments, and our self-image. On the psychic level, the solar plexus controls sensitivity to vibrations from other people and places. When the solar plexus is functioning properly we may experience radiance, warmth, awakening, transformation, and happiness. When the solar plexus is blocked or not working properly, we may take on more than we can handle at one time, experience power struggles with others, or feel anger, fear, or hate. A physical side effect of the solar plexus malfunctioning is to experience digestive problems. Gold also represents spiritual gifts.

Grapes

Grapes represent abundance and pleasure, and are seen on the King of Pentacles.

Hand

The right hand represents positive or masculine forces, which are generally associated with logic, rationality, and the sciences of mathematics and astronomy. The left hand represents negative or feminine forces that are generally associated with emotions, vibrational influences, intuition, and gut instincts. Two minor chakras located on the palms of the hands emanate energy from the body. These chakras on the palms of the hands are said to be directly linked to the heart chakra and perhaps this is the reason lovers can frequently be seen holding hands. A hand is seen on the Aces of Cups, Swords, Wands, and Pentacles.

Heart

The heart is associated with the heart chakra located at the center of the chest. In the heart chakra, the sensation of love is either expressed or blocked. When the heart chakra is functioning properly, we will generally experience unconditional love, forgiveness, compassion, balance, and oneness with life. When the heart chakra is blocked or malfunctioning, we may experience repressed love, emotional instability, and a general sense of imbalance. The physical side effects of an improperly working heart chakra are heart and circulation problems. The heart is seen in the Major Arcana on 3, The Empress.

Horse

Horses represent solar energy or the controlled, subdued life force. They represent strong forces or energies, and in Native American teaching they are considered to be very powerful beings. The domestication of horses enabled humanity to make a great leap forward in its evolution by providing a means of transport with the speed to travel greater distances and the strength to carry heavy loads. Before the use of the horse, humans were slow, heavy, earth-bound beings. When they were able to climb on the back of a horse, they were free and could carry heavy burdens over great distances. Humanity developed a special working relationship with the horse that altered their self-concept tremendously. The horse has had such a powerful impact on civilization that even today, power from engines is measured in *horsepower*. The horse is seen in the Major Arcana on 13, Death; and 19, The Sun.

House

A house is seen as a support mechanism to shield us from both manmade and natural elements that come into the atmosphere. The condition of the house is a reflection of the nature of the situation. Therefore, if the house is well built and furnished, then much stability is suggested, but if it is in need of repair there are important elements that need to be resolved before progress can be achieved. A house can be seen on the 10 of Pentacles and the 4 of Wands.

IHVH

IHIV, sometimes written as YHVH, is the Hebrew initial for Jehovah, who was often called "Jahwe" or "Jahve." Jehovah was the masculine monotheistic God of the ancient Hebrews. "I" represents the element of fire for which passion and energy come into being. "H" represents the element of water, which gives us sensitivity and emotions. "V" represents the element of air so that we have intellect and social awareness. The last "H" represents the element of earth, which gives us sensuality and groundedness. Interestingly enough, Yahweh sounds phonetically similar to Jupiter or Zeus, two gods who were considered to be prime forces in Greek and Roman mythology. IHVH can be seen in the Major Arcana on 10, Wheel of Fortune.

Iris

Iris is the Greek goddess of the rainbow, symbolizing God's grace and protection. It is a sign of blessing, goodness, and his love for the earth, and can be seen as a sign of peace after a storm. The iris appears in the Major Arcana on 14, Temperance.

Jewels

Jewels are an indication of opulence and success. They represent treasures and a sense of wholeness in us. Jewels can be seen on the 7 of Cups.

Keys Crossed

Keys represent access to something that is sought after. Keys can be seen as an opportunity to unlock some previously inaccessible potential or treasure. Crossed keys symbolize "keys to the kingdom," hidden doctrine, or secret esoteric teachings that first must be understood before they can be tapped into. The gold key represents the solar or masculine energy, while the silver represents the lunar or feminine energy. Keys are seen in the Major Arcana on 5, The Heirophant.

Lamp

Lamps are representative of enlightenment, awareness, insight, and perception. Lamps indicate spiritual light and perception. The lamp is seen on 9, The Hermit.

Leaves

Leaves represent growth and vitality, new starts, or a new chance in life. Leaves also represent healing forces. Leaves can be seen on 12, The Hanged Man.

Light

Light represents spiritual emanations or the activity of God. Light also represents spiritual illumination. If an area is well lit, there is much illumination, but if surroundings are dim, more needs to be discovered about the situation in question. In many occult teachings light is seen as alive and intelligent, which both conceives and sustains creation. Devas and angels are said to live and reside in the light. In modern technology, the harnessing and use of light has become a powerful medium that is used for communication such as fiber optic technology, solar energy, healing, and even destruction;

lasers are believed to have been the downfall of the advanced civilization of Atlantis.

Lightning
Lightning is seen as a flash of inspiration, which flashes help us to understand the problem we are dealing with at the time. Lightning can also be a signal to alert us of an upcoming storm. It is thought to be the life-power that descends down to the Cabalistic Tree of Life. Lightning can be seen on 16, The Tower.

Lily
The lily is considered an abstract thought that hasn't been tinged with lust or desires. The lily is seen in the Major Arcana in 1, The Magician.

Lion
The lion is the king of the beasts and represents the astrological sign of Leo. The lion is royal, dynamic, and magnanimous, a proud and glamorous being who is strong and warm. In Native American teachings, the lion is a leader. Because the lion is the leader, it is often placed in a position to be a target for the problems of others. When no one wants to, or cannot take the lead, the lion will take charge of the situation, but is then often blamed when things go wrong. Therefore, before the lion is fully evolved, it must learn many lessons about the proper use of power, and how to lead without insisting others follow. The lion is also a hunter, but it is the female lion that hunts, and she only takes what she and her family need. The lion is seen in the Major Arcana on 8, Strength; 10, Wheel of Fortune; and 21, The World.

Moon

The Moon rules the astrological sign of Cancer and represents emotions and feelings. Before the discovery of the planet Neptune in the nineteenth century, the Moon also ruled the subconscious mind and psychic abilities. The Moon is feminine in nature and represents women in general, motherhood, water, emotions, and intuition. The Moon is seen in the Major Arcana on 2, The High Priestess; and 18, The Moon.

Mountains

Mountains represent wisdom and understanding. They denote being in a higher state of consciousness and closer to God. Mountains also represent clear, rational thinking and the height of abstract thought. Mountains can at times represent a barrier we must overcome or a pinnacle we must reach.

Orb of the World

The orb of the world is a traditional symbol of the earth dominated by the Lord. A more modern interpretation of this symbol is that it is the sphere of our experience, our own world of awareness and activity, or the way in which we experience the world. The orb of the world can be seen in the Major Arcana on 4, The Emperor.

Palm Tree

The palm tree is a symbol for victory over death. It is seen as the male aspect of life. The palm is an active force and represents the unfolding of spiritual forces. The palm tree, being masculine, is found in the Major Arcana on 2, The High

Priestess. The palm leaf is also a crucial symbol in Christianity as the Sunday before Easter is celebrated as Palm Sunday, commemorating Jesus the Christ's entry into Jerusalem five days before his crucifixion. When Jesus entered Jerusalem, the people of the city laid palm leaves in his path as a sign of welcome. The palm on this card seems to neutralize the femininity inherent in the archetype that the card depicts, and reinforces the idea that the High Priestess is celibate.

Path

The path is seen as a way of progressing in our spiritual evolution. It is the method we choose to take on our journey to self-discovery, increased self-awareness, and a deeper participation in life. When surmounted by one obstacle after another, we need to look closely at the path we are on because it may not be taking us where we need to go. Paths can be seen in the Major Arcana on 14, Temperance; and 18, The Moon.

Pentacle

The pentacle is a five-pointed star, or pentagram, which has been fashioned into an amulet. It is an ancient symbol used to describe the five stages required to transform animal nature into true humanhood. In the Tarot, the pentacle represents the element of earth, so it is primarily concerned with work, money, sensuality, and fertility. When the pentacle is in the form of an amulet, it is said to protect us against evil spirits. When the pentacle is upside down, it represents the exploitation and glorification of animal drives and erotic forces. The pentacle is seen in the Major Arcana in 15, The Devil.

Pillar

Pillars provide support, backing, and balance. When the pillars are colored, the white represents positive energies and the black represents negative. Together the two pillars provide an equal balance. When looking at the two pillars, it is important to note whether we are drawn to one over the other, which could indicate there is an imbalance somewhere in our lives. Pillars are seen in the Major Arcana on 2, The High Priestess; 5, The Heirophant; and 11, Justice.

Pleiades

In astronomy this is a loose cluster of 400 to 500 stars in the constellation of Taurus, about 415 light years from our own solar system. In Greek mythology these stars are the seven daughters of Atlas and Pleione. There are several stories concerning these mythical beings, but one version is that they are the attendants of Artemis, god of wildlife and hunting, and were pursued by the giant hunter Orion, but were rescued by the gods and changed into doves. After their death, or metamorphosis, they were transformed into stars, but are nonetheless still pursued across the sky by the constellation Orion. The Pleiades can be seen on 17, The Star.

Pomegranates

The pomegranate is a symbol of fertility, passivity, and receptivity. The pomegranate is shown in the Major Arcana on 2, The High Priestess.

Pyramid

The pyramid is seen as the earth in its maternal aspect. The triangular shape of the pyramid suggests the three-fold principle of creation. More modern meanings of the pyramid are a wider awareness or integration of the self, or death of some sort. Pyramids are said to have higher vibrations and much spiritual power. Many people use pyramids as aids in meditation and healing. A pyramid can be seen on the Knight of Wands.

Rabbit

The rabbit is considered to be a symbol of fertility. In Native American teachings, the rabbit is the symbol for fear and is called the "Fear Caller" because he calls his fear to him so that it can become reality. Rabbits signify sexual prowess, quick changes of partners, and fast multiplication of offspring. A rabbit can be seen on the Queen of Pentacles.

Rainbow

The rainbow is a sign from God of future protection and happiness. In the Old Testament, the rainbow was considered to be a covenant between God and humanity that he would never again send a flood to destroy the earth. The rainbow is also seen as peace after the storm and God's grace. The rainbow is seen on the 10 of Cups.

Ram's Head

The ram's head is the symbol for the planet Mars and the astrological sign of Aries. The ram symbolizes leadership, which is often achieved through force. Aries is the sign of the conqueror who wants to be first and have it all. While Leo is in a position of leadership because of his regal persona, Aries leads because he has the prowess to pursue and take what he wants. The ram's head is seen in the Major Arcana on 4, The Emperor.

Rose

Roses symbolize beauty. Some people interpret roses to mean sexuality, with the bud of the rose depicting either the male or female sexual organs. Since roses must be cultivated, they generally represent cultural activities. The white rose symbolizes freedom from lower forms of desire and passion, while the red rose represents Venus, nature, or desire. Roses are seen in the Major Arcana on 0, The Fool; and 1, The Magician.

Salamander

The salamander is a mythical lizardlike animal that has the ability to endure fire without harm. This being represents the suit of Wands because of its fiery qualities. The salamander can be seen on the court cards in the suit of Wands.

Scales

Scales symbolize balance, judgment, karma, harmony, and fairness. Scales are the symbol for the astrological sign of Libra. Libra tries to maintain equilibrium, but even a tiny feather added to one side of the scale is enough to bring it completely out of balance. Scales can be seen in the Major Arcana on 11, Justice.

Scroll

A scroll is represented by divine law and the hidden mysteries. Scrolls have been mentioned many times in biblical prophecy. The prophets Ezekiel, Zechariah, and John had several encounters with beings that showed them scrolls in several fashions. From biblical accounts alone, it is apparent that scrolls contain only the most sacred material and are serious communicating devices. The scroll is seen in the Major Arcana on 2, The High Priestess.

Serpent

The serpent is seen as a symbol of wisdom, secrecy, and subtlety. The serpent is one of the symbols for the astrological sign of Scorpio because of its reptilian ability to transform and regenerate yearly through shedding its skin. The root chakra is symbolically depicted as a serpent asleep at the base of the spine. This sleeping serpent is called the kundalini. When the kundalini is stimulated, the serpent travels up from the base of the spine, all the way to the crown chakra. In Native American teachings the snake is seen as a symbol of transmutation because it sheds its skin once each year. The snake is enigmatic as it embodies sexuality, psychic energy, alchemy, reproduction, and immortality. In the Bible, the serpent is the only animal cunning enough to trick Eve into eating of the forbidden fruit. Although the serpent is seen as evil in the Genesis account by many, some Bible scholars postulate that the serpent didn't trick Eve, but was actually symbolic of the kundalini energy awakening within the couple. Even the Bible depicts the serpent as a powerful being who had healing and transforming capabilities. When Moses was in the desert with the Israelites, poisonous snakes invaded the camp. Moses was instructed by Jehovah to make a bronze serpent and place it on a pole so that anyone who was bitten by a snake only had to look at the bronze serpent to survive. Even to this day the medical profession has chosen to use the serpent as a symbol for its profession, thus verifying its healing qualities. The serpent is seen in the Major Arcana on 6, The Lovers; and 10, Wheel of Fortune.

Shellfish

The shellfish symbolizes the early stages of conscious unfoldment. Shellfish can also symbolize the defensive shell we build up around ourselves to avoid hurt, or sexual or emotional involvement. Shellfish are seen in the Major Arcana on 18, The Moon.

Ship

Ships depict a spiritual vehicle, body, or progress. A ship can depict a voyage in life, the soul's journey, or the path we are presently taking. Ships can also denote spiritual pleasure, leisure, or gain. The ship can be seen on the 2 of Pentacles.

Silver

Silver is the metal associated with the Moon. It is a precious metal that is considered by many to have esoteric implications.

Sphinx

The sphinx is symbolically known as the "dweller on the threshold," and represents fears, illusions, or bad habits we wish to be free of. The sphinx is said to be a guardian of all that is sacred, or the ancient mysteries. It is considered to be a being in the same order as an angel, and a great mystery school is believed to have been located in the immediate vicinity to the Great Sphinx in Egypt. In mythology, the sphinx is a combination of human and animal attributes. In the Tarot, the white sphinx symbolizes mercy while the black symbolizes severity. The sphinx is seen in the Major Arcana on 7, The Chariot; and 10, Wheel of Fortune.

Square

In astrology the square is a 90-degree angle between two planets. This angle puts conflict and challenge into the life of the native where the planet, sign, and house of the square occur. Four perfect squares that form two 180-degree oppositions to each other constitute a Grand Square, which is relatively rare in a horoscope. The Grand Square brings many problems, trials, and lessons to be learned to help us become stronger. If the native is able to face and overcome these life challenges imposed by the Grand Square, he will be endowed with great strength and power. The four corners of the square symbolize the number four in numerology, so it gives four solidity, practicality, and a sense of earthiness. The square is seen on 14, Temperance.

Staff

The staff is a symbol of honor, profession, authority, or power. It is an implement used by Moses in biblical accounts, the Magician in the Tarot, the bishop in the church, and the shepherd when watching his flocks. The staff is seen on 9, The Hermit.

Star

The star is a point of illumination representing our hopes, ideals, or messages from other realms. Stars generally depict love, peace, compassion, and spiritual perfection. In biblical times a star and a planet were considered the same. The

Morning or Evening Star, as referenced in the Bible, is actually the planet Venus. The star that the Magi, or astrologers, used to predict the exact date, time, and place of Jesus the Christ's birth was actually the triple conjunction of Jupiter and Saturn over an eight-month time frame, which occurs only once every 800 years. The star can be seen in the Major Arcana on 9, The Hermit; and 17, The Star.

Stone

Stones are undoubtedly the oldest beings on earth today and have been around since the creation of our earth. Stones have seen every age, era, war, and evolvement of humankind. The Native Americans have great respect for these ageless beings and call them the Stone People. The history of the world is said to be recorded into their lines and cracks. The information is ours only for the asking, but we need to develop our intuitive skills before the Stone People will speak to us. Stone People also have great healing and grounding properties. When we feel nervous, tense, agitated, or hurried we are not properly grounded to the earth. Since Stone People are so close to the earth, we only need to hold one in our hands and breathe quietly with the rhythm of the earth to restore our balance and harmony. The stone can be seen on 14, Temperance.

Stream

Streams portray a flow of emotion, ideas, or information and are considered a source of spiritual refreshment, which flows into the ocean of cosmic consciousness.

Sun

The Sun is the source of light and the giver of life in our solar system. Without the life-giving energy from the Sun, there would be no life here on earth, as we know it. In astrology, the Sun represents the life force, basic character, or ego of the native. While the Sun is the center of our solar system, in astrology it usually indicates the center of attention. The Sun represents love, romance, creativity, enjoyment and children. The Sun is seen in the Major Arcana on 0, The Fool; 6, The Lovers; 13, Death; and 19, The Sun.

Sunflowers

Sunflowers traditionally follow the Sun's light. Sunflowers represent nature in its fullness, abundance, sunshine, a sunny disposition, and prosperity. Sunflowers can be seen on 19, The Sun.

Swords

Swords represent activity that can be either constructive or destructive. Swords can symbolize great power and decisiveness, as witnessed when a king or queen knights someone. Swords have much spiritual power, which can be used to accomplish what is thought impossible. A two-edged sword indicates that it can cut both ways. For this reason, if we intend to inflict damage on another we need to make sure we will not damage ourselves as well. Swords also represent the law and can be used to eliminate outdated ideas and practices. Swords represent the element of air, and possess many mental and social qualities. Swords are seen in the Major Arcana on 11, Justice.

Sylph

The sylph is an elemental being said to inhabit the element of air. The sylph is associated with the suit of Swords.

Tower

The tower, as depicted in the Genesis account of the Tower of Babel, is humanity's creation to help them move closer to God. If the tower is built on a false science or shaky foundation, it will easily come down or be destroyed. It can represent a higher consciousness or viewpoint, but can also depict a false sense of security. The tower is seen in the Major Arcana on 13, Death; 16, The Tower; and 18, The Moon.

Tree

There are two trees primary to the Tarot. The first is the Tree of Knowledge of Good and Evil, which bears five fruits to represent the five senses. The second is the Tree of Life, which bears twelve fruits to represent the twelve signs of the zodiac. Trees depict structure in our inner self. The roots reach down into the earth to keep us grounded, while the branches extend to the sky to help us link with God. Native Americans believe trees have much energy because of their size and age. When we are feeling sapped of energy and tired of the hustle and bustle of the world, we only need to sit next to the tree and it will gladly give us the energy and tranquility we need to recenter ourselves. Trees breathe carbon dioxide and exhale oxygen while humans breathe oxygen and exhale carbon dioxide, thus creating interdependence between the animal and plant kingdom. Trees also symbolize new growth or stages of life and death. Trees can be seen in the Major Arcana on 6, The Lovers.

Trumpet

A trumpet indicates that an important message is coming soon. The trumpet can be seen on 20, Judgement.

Undine

An undine is an elemental being that lives in water and is associated with the suit of Cups. The undine can be seen on the throne of the Queen of Cups.

Veils

Veils signify things that are hidden. The veil allows us to vaguely see what is behind it, adding a touch of mystique to the subject at hand. In order to fully see what is behind the veil, it must first be lifted. After the veil has been lifted, the reality of the situation may not be what we had perceived it to be. In biblical accounts, Laban deceived Jacob into marrying his eldest daughter Leah, instead of his younger daughter Rachel. One of the ways Laban was able to succeed in his deception was to cover and veil Leah so Jacob could not tell the difference between the two women. Veils present an illusion that may not accurately depict the entire situation. As veils to our subconscious are lifted, we are able to see more clearly about life, death, and truth. It is said that our conscious awareness is veiled to enable us to only see what we need to see and view time in a quite restricted fashion. If we were able to tap into all of the information that is actually in existence, it would inhibit our soul growth by making many of us unable to deal with the present, and deter us in our earth walk. The veil is seen in the Major Arcana on 2, The High Priestess; and 11, Justice.

Wand

Wands represent will, magic, power, and transformation. Wands use spiritual forces for good, and are often used to perform miracles. Some wands are perceived as phallic symbols. The wand is representative of the element of fire and is depicted in the suit of Wands in the Minor Arcana. The wand is seen in the Major Arcana on 21, The World.

Water

Water symbolizes the subconscious and our emotional state. Water is the source of all life and symbolizes life-giving energies and the spiritual flow of truth, knowledge, healing, or refreshment. The state or condition of the water is a good indication of the state of our being. If the water is calm and clear, we are likely to be serene. If, however, the water is turbulent, we may be experiencing some emotional troubles at this time. Water is representative of the suit of Cups in the Minor Arcana. Water is seen in the Major Arcana on 14, Temperance; 17, The Star; 18, The Moon; and 20, Judgement.

Water Lilies

Water lilies represent peaceful emotions and eternal life. Water lilies are seen on the Ace of Cups.

Wheat

Wheat represents abundance and fertility, and is considered a sacred life essence. Wheat also symbolizes wisdom and the harvest of life experiences. Wheat can be seen on 3, The Empress.

Wheel

The wheel symbolizes the cycle of life or cosmic expression. The center of the wheel depicts the world when it was just a thought or idea. The inner circle of the wheel represents the creation of the world. The outer circle represents the world as it materializes, and the spokes of the wheel are a means to channel universal energy to the material world. The wheel is seen in the Major Arcana on 7, The Chariot; and 10, Wheel of Fortune.

Window

A window acts as a view to the world of others for what could be. Quite often people can be caught looking out of windows when daydreaming of a better life or wondering about the activities of others. A window can be seen in the 5 of Pentacles.

Wolf

In Native American teachings, the wolf is the teacher of the animal kingdom. Wolves are very social animals, and their family and social structures are quite like humans. Wolves select one partner and mate for life. They are loyal like dogs, which are actually domesticated animals bred from the wolf. Wolves are very socially oriented, but at the same time possess their own individuality. Since the wolf's social milieu is so close to humans', this animal can teach us much about the world in which we live. The wolf, being wild, also symbolizes nature before it has been tamed and civilized by man. The wolf is seen in the Major Arcana on 18, The Moon.

Wreath

The wreath represents the forces of nature and the harvested plant kingdom of life. The wreath is seen in the Major Arcana on 3, The Empress; 8, Strength; and 21, The World.

YOD (drops of light)

The YOD is called the Finger of God. It is an extremely powerful astrological aspect composed of three planets combined to produce two 150-degree angles and one 60-degree angle. The YOD usually lies dormant until a transit or progression triggers it into action. When the power YOD is awakened from its slumber, it exacts a major force or decision that leaves the life of the native never quite the same again. The YOD is seen in the Major Arcana on 16, The Tower; and 18, The Moon.

Zero

Zero is a very powerful number, ruled by the planet Pluto and the astrological sign of Scorpio. Before the advent of the number zero, humankind's analytical ability to form complex mathematical concepts was somewhat limited, but zero changed all that, and allowed man to advance in his technological evolution. Zero is the symbol of nothingness and denotes freedom from limitations in this material world. Zero is seen in the Major Arcana on 0, The Fool.

Zodiac

The zodiac is the symbol of the cycle of existence. It is a circle, with twelve segments called signs. Each sign depicts a certain personality type or trait. All twelve signs, when combined, form completeness.

NUMEROLOGY AND THE TAROT

Numerology is the study of numbers and the impact they play on our lives, as well as the frequency in which they appear. A basic understanding of how numbers relate to specific cards in Tarot is essential because it helps to shed further illumination on the meaning of each card.

In the study of numerology, numbers 1 through 9 are considered to be primary numbers and any numbers higher than 9 are considered to be compound. Compound numbers are derived because they comprise qualities of all of the numbers, which they contain, as well as the overall number, which is derived when they are added together. For example, the number 27 is computed by adding the digits in the number together (2 + 7) to come up with the primary number 9. The number 27 will also carry the secondary vibrations of 2 and 7 in addition to the main vibration of 9. Therefore, although 27 is a higher octave of 9, its vibrations are subtly different from other compound numbers that also add up to 9, such as 45 or 36.

Some numerologists do not include zero when analyzing numbers and this is a shame because it is a powerful number that helps to further enlighten us to some of the rather profound occurrences that happen in our lives. When using numerology with the Tarot, zero is important because it represents The Fool in the Major Arcana and makes up the compound number of ten in the Minor Arcana.

Single Digit Numbers

Zero

Zero is a powerful number representing transformation. Zero's power is so intense that it causes overwhelming events to occur in the lives of those who cross its path. Zero is ruled by the planet Pluto and the astrological sign of Scorpio. Positively, zero is deep, intense, and healing. Negatively, it is compulsive, extreme, and vindictive.

One

One is the beginning of the cycle. It is where creation begins and it is quite dynamic. This number is full of authority, power, and leadership. One is ruled by the Sun and the astrological sign of Leo. Positively, one is dramatic, creative, romantic, and childishly enthusiastic. Negatively, it is egocentric, bossy, and selfish.

Two

Two represents balance. It is receptive, feminine, and would like to care for and be cared for by others. This is a sensitive number, which is wholesome. Two is ruled by the Moon and the astrological sign of Cancer. Positively, two is sensitive, caring, and nurturing. Negatively, it is grasping, moody, and irritable.

Three

Three represents expansion. It is wise, understanding, scholarly, and yearns to travel to foreign lands in order to experience life to the fullest. Three is the number of the higher intellect and is therefore prominently placed in the lives of teachers and professionals. Three is ruled by the planet Jupiter and the astrological sign of Sagittarius. Positively, three is optimistic, understanding, and philosophical. Negatively, it takes unnecessary risks, behaves foolishly, and can be pessimistic.

Four

Four is a complex number. Many believe four represents stability, hard work, and building foundations. This may be so, but four also craves change and may be the culprit behind many a revolution. Some texts state that four is ruled by the more negative aspects of the Sun while others state that it is ruled by Uranus and the astrological sign Aquarius. There is a school of thought that teaches that four's true ruler is actually Mars, and this seems to be more accurate when working the Tarot because the fourth card in the Major Arcana is The Emperor, which is more closely aligned with Mars and Aries. Positively, four is stable, unique, and inventive. Negatively, it is egocentric, aggressive, and demanding.

Five

Five can be seen as intellectual, communicative, and analytical. It deals with learning, education, and communication. Five is ruled by the planet Mercury and the astrological signs of Gemini and Virgo. Positively, five is versatile, witty, and quick thinking. Negatively, it is nervous, gossipy, and overly critical.

Six

Six seeks balance, harmony, and beauty. Six likes one-to-one relationships and has a strong sense of justice. Six is charming and prefers to be surrounded by luxury. Six is ruled by the planet Venus and the astrological signs of Taurus and Libra. Positively, six is fertile, charming, and balanced. Negatively, it is judgmental, obstinate, shallow, and jealous.

Seven

Seven is a dreamer that needs to take care not to live in a fantasy world. Seven is so sensitive that it is highly intuitive and even psychic. Seven has such high ideals that it may at times live in an unrealistic, vague dream world. Seven is ruled by the planet Neptune and the astrological sign of Pisces. Positively, seven is compassionate, spiritual, and psychic. Negatively, it is sacrificial and delusional.

Eight

Eight is a workhorse that gives structure and stability to our lives through hard work. Eight is often forced to learn by experience or from its own mistakes; as a consequence it is somewhat of a disciplinarian and can be at times stern. This number can be difficult to live with because it is said to represent our karma in life. Wherever eight appears we will be forced to mature and deal with issues from the past. Eight is ruled by the planet Saturn and the astrological sign of Capricorn. Positively, eight is responsible, dedicated, and ambitious. Negatively, it is fearful, cautious, and strict.

Nine

Nine has a great deal of energy and seeks excitement so that it can gain greater wisdom from these experiences. Nine can be rather assertive, even to the point of being aggressive. Nine is very ardent when it comes to exploring unconquered territory. In ancient times, nine was considered sacred and represented the completion of a cycle. This sense of completion is exemplified by the fact that it takes nine months to bring a baby to life from the time of its original conception. Some believe nine to be ruled by the planet Mars because of its capacity for growth, but it also carries with it Uranian characteristics because it heralds vast changes wherever it appears. Additionally, in the Major Arcana, nine is represented by The Hermit, who is somewhat of a loner—this independent solitude is more typical of an Aquarian type than an Arian. It is possible that nine could very well have been ruled by Mars before the discovery of Uranus, but this new planet's entrance into our conscious awareness has given the sacred number a new ruler. Positively, nine is assertive, enthusiastic, and exploring. Negatively, it is temperamental, accidental, and aggressive.

Compound Numbers

Ten

Ten is a powerful number, representing the end of the cycle of numbers used in the Minor Arcana, and therefore signifying completion. This completion is also represented in the fact that it takes ten lunar months to bring a baby to life from the time of its original conception, and the fact that our primary number system in use today is based on ten digits. It should not be forgotten that ten has its roots in antiquity where God presented Moses with the Ten Commandments. Ten has much self-confidence, and emanates love and light. Ten is a compound number and therefore carries with it the creative vibration of one and the healing vibration of zero. Positively, ten is complete, fully developed, and gifted. Negatively, it is extreme, overconfident, and abuses power.

Eleven

Eleven is a higher octave of the number two and is considered to be a master number that has mystical properties. Because eleven is a master number, it also has the propensity for hidden treachery and therefore a balance between good and evil needs to be maintained when working with such numbers. Eleven often represents two people of the same or opposite sex who are in conflict with each other and therefore need to unite before they can achieve harmony or individuality.

Twelve

Twelve is also considered a master number, and is a higher octave of the number three. Twelve signifies completion because there are twelve months in the year, twelve signs in the zodiac, twelve apostles of Christ, and the twelve tribes of Israel, just to name a few of the significant occurrences of this number throughout our history. Because twelve is considered to be a master number, it also carries hidden threats. The number twelve is often associated with sacrifice and victimization, so continual alertness is a must when this number appears.

Thirteen

Thirteen is a higher octave of the number four. It is not unlucky as some might suggest, but merely symbolizes the destruction that can occur when power is wrongly used. Thirteen is one more than twelve—the number of completion. It symbolizes power, regeneration, and the need to adapt to change gracefully.

Fourteen

Fourteen is a higher octave of the number five and represents challenge. Fourteen symbolizes danger overcome, especially in natural disasters. With fourteen, intuition needs to be relied upon and heeded when making decisions.

Fifteen

Fifteen is a higher octave of the number six and represents personal magnetism. Fifteen is a fortunate number for acquiring money. However, selfishness, materialism, and obstinacy should be avoided.

Sixteen

Sixteen is a higher octave of the number seven and is associated with danger, which is primarily caused by overconfidence. With sixteen, it is best to pay careful attention to detail and trust the inner voice.

Seventeen

Seventeen is a higher octave of the number eight and is associated with harmony, spirituality, love, and peace. Seventeen has the ability to conquer failed relationships.

Eighteen

Eighteen is a higher octave of the number nine and can be a difficult number to live with. With this number, the conflict between spirituality and materialism is ever present. Quarrels with family or friends are common, and friends and enemies may be guilty of deception. Meeting hatred and deception from others with love and forgiveness can dilute the negative effects of this number.

Nineteen

Nineteen is a higher octave of the number one and is considered to be fortunate. It is the number of goodness and represents victory over disappointment and general success in life.

Twenty

Twenty is a higher octave of the number two and represents awakening, resurrection or rebirth, which brings about a new purpose in life. This number carries with it psychic potential in the form of precognitive dreams. Faith needs to be cultivated with this number.

Twenty-one

Twenty-one is a higher octave of the number three and is a positive number, which signifies advancement and indicates victory after a long struggle. Twenty-one is considered to be a karmic reward and indicates freedom, independence, and achieved ambitions. This number also signifies that a major cycle has been completed, so new paths must soon begin to continue on the spiritual journey.

The Cyclic Rhythm of the Tarot

Everything in life has a cycle, consisting of a beginning and an end. Sometimes there can be a rebirth within the middle of the cycle which will lead to a new beginning, thus initiating a new cycle altogether. The Tarot was designed to represent the entire cyclic rhythm of our lives, with the Major Arcana incrementing twenty-two stages in the more meaningful implications of our lives, while each suit of the Minor Arcana contains ten stages and four lesser stages, totaling fourteen.

When we are in the middle of a cycle, it need not progress in a linear fashion, but can go backward, forward, and even sidestep stages to encompass separate but related issues. Because the cycles we encounter sometimes seem to have no set pattern, it can be difficult to ascertain the beginning and end of each one. Each person who enters into a cycle does so at a different level of awareness and will progress through the cycle at his own pace. Therefore, two people who enter a cycle at the same time, place, and emotional level may not necessary complete the cycle via the same routes, thus explaining why many people choose to end relationships simply because they have grown apart and find that they no longer have anything in common. A person can travel many pathways to complete a cycle, and the Tarot attempts to depict many such avenues. Every cycle we enter into must be completed, and we cannot jump out of the cycle in the middle of an evolutionary process merely because we do not like what is occurring. These are necessary to our development and must be completed before we can move into other spiritual levels.

8

ELEMENTAL ASTROLOGY
AND THE TAROT

In the Western world we identify with four basic elements that help us relate to concepts, people, places, and things. Elements were used as the principle building blocks when Tarot, astrology, and other esoteric sciences were initially designed. The four elements the Western world currently identifies with are fire, earth, air, and water, with each element corresponding to a suit in the Minor Arcana. The element of spirit, which is not included in the traditional grouping, corresponds with the Major Arcana.

Fire

Fire is considered to be a life force, which gives zest to our lives. Fire is active, adventurous, and aggressive, as well as playful, creative, and loving. Fire wants to be first and it should therefore come as no surprise to discover that many people with a preponderance of fire in their birth horoscopes tend to think primarily of their own wants, needs, and desires. In matters of love, fire is conquering, exciting, and romantic. Fire is associated with the astrological signs of

Aries, Leo, and Sagittarius, and the suit of Wands identifies most closely with this element. Because fire is so swift, in terms of time, it relates to days. Therefore, each numbered card in the suit of Wands will equate to the number on the card multiplied by one day.

Earth

Earth is the stabilizing force in our lives, which reminds us of our duties, responsibilities, and obligations, and thus helps us to achieve our worldly ambitions. Earth helps us to work, earn money, and advance in our careers. Because of this emphasis on materialism, earth can at times appear boring or greedy, but it can also be very sensual and enjoys good food, drink, and pleasurable entertainment. In matters of love, earth tends to be more analytical, practical, and sensual, and will choose a partner based on what he or she can bring into the family unit rather than allow infatuation to get in the way of making a logical decision. Earth is associated with the astrological signs of Taurus, Virgo, and Capricorn, and the suit of Pentacles identifies most closely with this element. Because earth is somewhat slower than the other elements, in terms of time each numbered card in the suit of Pentacles will equate to the number on the card multiplied by one month.

Air

Air is intellectual and wants to think, communicate, and socialize. Air is responsible for the development of acquaintanceships, close relationships, and marriages. Air likes to be surrounded by friends and needs a wide variety of intellectual stimulation or it will soon become bored. In matters of love, air tends to prefer any commitments to be cemented with a legal contract because it knows all too well that verbal arrangements can easily be misunderstood. Air is associated with the astrological signs of Gemini, Libra, and Aquarius, and the suit of Swords identifies most closely with this element. In terms of time, this element relates to the fortnight. Therefore, each numbered card in the suit of Swords will equate to the number on the card multiplied by one fortnight.

Water

Water gives us feelings that can range from pure, to intense, to spiritual in nature. Without water, we cannot feel, as this element is often highly intuitive and can easily escape into a fantasy world of addiction if other stabilizing forces are not present. Water is an elusive element and is often responsible for delusion in our lives. In matters of love, water seeks soul-mate relationships that are intense and spiritual. Water is associated with the astrological signs of Cancer, Scorpio, and Pisces, and the suit of Cups most closely identifies with this element. In terms of time, this element relates to the week. Therefore, each numbered card in the suit of Cups will equate to the number on the card multiplied by one week.

Spirit

The element of spirit is associated with the higher, more karmic realms of our daily lives. Spirit cannot adequately be portrayed within the confines of the four elements of fire, earth, air, or water because it transcends day-to-day activities. The element of spirit normally indicates that we are going into deeper, more meaningful levels of reality. This element most closely identifies with the Major Arcana. Because matters of the spirit as a general rule tend to transcend time and space, they affect our lives in such a transformative way that in terms of time it equates to one year. Therefore, the duration of each card in the Major Arcana will equate to the number on the card multiplied by one year.

How The Elements and Suits Relate to One Another

When one element is combined with another, these two elements form a reaction, which can result in either a positive, negative, or neutral effect. For example, the elements of earth/Pentacles and water/Cups are said to compliment each other and provide a favorable influence because emotional water pours forth onto practical earth to provide much needed, life-giving moisture, which will later bring forth vegetation and life. However, if these same watery emotions overflow and flood the earth, the same moisture can saturate and drown the plants it had previously helped give life to. Therefore, the compatibility of elements should never be taken for granted, and one should never assume that earth is always compatible with water and that air is always incompatible with water. While these generalizations help to simplify things for people who do not understand the intricate workings of elemental forces, the serious student of the esoteric arts should always look deeper into these issues and avoid generalizations.

The Element of Fire or
The Suit of Wands

Fire Combined with Fire

Fire coupled with fire has a neutral effect on most occasions. When the elements of fire are combined, this indicates that much energy is put forth into business matters. Although fire when combined with itself is said to be beneficial, too much fire can become explosive. For this reason it is essential to properly use the vast amount of energy inherent in the suit of Wands or the element of fire.

Fire Combined with Air

The element of air tends to strengthen fire. The creative energy of fire coupled with the mental agility of air brings much mental creation in the form of visions and ideas. When a touch of air is blown onto a burning ember the flame will intensify and strengthen. However, if a huge gust of air overpowers that same ember, it will extinguish the flame. Therefore, it is always necessary to temper air and fire so that these two elements can enhance each other.

Fire Combined with Earth

When fire is coupled with earth, these two elements have the effect of complimenting each other. The energy inherent in fire mingled with the practicality of earth helps us to achieve our materialistic goals through hard work. As with the other elements, fire's energy needs to be properly directed so that it doesn't scorch the practical potential of earth.

Fire Combined with Water

When fire is mixed with water much care needs to be taken to ensure that these elements do not weaken each other. When emotions are mixed with energy, a melodramatic emotional outburst can occur if a proper balance is not maintained. The activators inherent in fire can generate much creativity when combined with the sensitivity of water.

The Element of Earth or
The Suit of Pentacles

Earth Combined with Earth

When earth is combined with itself it has a somewhat neutral influence. The two earthy elements have a tendency to reinforce each other's practical qualities so money, property, and other basal concerns predominate. Although earth coupled with it is usually neutral, too much earth can lead to excessive materialism, possessiveness, greed, or lust.

Earth Combined with Water

The element of earth combined with water has somewhat of a neutral impact when coupled together. The practicality of earth generally has the effect of stabilizing water's deeply flowing emotions. Earth helps water to keep its deep emotions in check. Although the astrological sign of Capricorn is considered to be of the earthy element, the fact that the symbol is half fish and half goat indicates that this sign, at least on an esoteric level, has deeply buried emotions that have somehow been transcended to form more highly rationalized thought processes. Excavations of ancient oriental drawings also suggest that the earthly sign of Capricorn was at one time a water element. Additionally, our modern zodiac was not in its present form until about 2,000 years ago, when it is said that Julius Caesar carved Libra and Virgo out of the former great snake-like constellation of Scorpio in an effort to make the calendar more accurate. With this in mind, Capricorn may well have been considered more emotive than present-day astrologers give it credit for, and these ancient influences may still lie dormant in our zodiac's most serious sign. When earth is combined with water the creativity channeled through is more useful. These two elements combined together tend to focus on realistic emotions and feelings toward family and possessions.

Earth Combined with Air

When earth is coupled with air, the influence of these two elements can be weakened. The intellectual influences of air combined with earth can produce a conflict of material versus mental concerns, or analytical thought processes versus reality.

The Element of Air or The Suit of Swords

The suit of Swords is symbolic of air, and unfortunately many of the cards in this suit depict strife and discord. This relates to the fact that the honing of communication skills is of paramount importance to prevent misunderstandings. Most wars, arguments, and other such conflicts occur simply because people are not able to communicate their needs effectively.

Air Combined with Air

When air is coupled with itself it generally has a somewhat neutral effect. Because air is mentally agile, the combination of these two elements stimulates a great deal of cerebral activity. This mental activity can take the form of correspondence, writing, and decision making. Since air generally dictates verbal activity, misunderstanding and discord can sometimes occur.

Air Combined with Water

When air is coupled with water, these two elements have a tendency to strengthen one another. The intellectual characteristics of air mingled with the emotional sensitivity of water tend to produce creative ideas. A touch of water mixed with air can form a fine mist, which creates a sense of refreshing coolness on a warm day. However, if that same water becomes too heavy, the mist will give way to heavy humidity or showers. For this reason, it is essential that just the right amount of water be mingled with air to ensure a positive outcome.

The Element of Water or The Suit of Cups

Water Combined with Water

When water is coupled with itself, it tends to have a somewhat neutral effect. Water mixed with itself highlights emotional sensitivity. If this emotional sensitivity is positive, much joy, love, fun, and creativity can come from the union. However, if the emotions are low, then excessive fantasy or depression can result.

9

ASTROLOGY AND THE TAROT

Concepts of astrology were used in the design of the Tarot, with the subtle symbolism and characteristics enmeshed in each card. Each card in the Tarot is assigned a specific astrological planet or sign to help provide greater clarity when reading the oracle.

A basic understanding of the traditional planets, signs, and houses will immensely aid the student of Tarot and help to speed up the learning process which must inevitably transpire for one to become proficient at this art.

Planets

Planets are considered celestial bodies that orbit the zodiac and vibrate at their own unique frequency to affect different areas of our lives. Many astrologers have also begun to include some of the larger asteroids in their astrological interpretations because these bodies tend to present more refined psychological influences, which are becoming more apparent in our increasingly complicated lifestyles. Although the Sun and Moon are technically not planets, they are classified as such because they too are celestial bodies that appear to encircle the zodiac when using geocentric, or earth-centered astrology. The nodes of the Moon, while not actual planets themselves, have an important influence and are also taken into consideration when delineating a natal horoscope.

The Sun

The Sun is the center of our solar system—without its life-giving light and heat there would be no life on earth as we know it. The Sun is happy, vibrant, and romantic. It displays childlike enthusiasm, and represents the basic nature of a person. In astrology, the Sun rules Leo and the fifth house of the horoscope. In Tarot, it rules The Sun in the Major Arcana, and 4, 5, and 6 of Wands in the Minor Arcana.

The Moon

The Moon is the largest satellite to orbit the Earth and represents feelings and emotional reactions. It is intuitive, sensitive, and often symbolizes mother figures. The Moon is very protective and nurturing, so it may at times cling to persons or situations when it should just let go. In astrology, the Moon rules Cancer and the fourth house. In Tarot the Moon rules the High Priestess and The Moon in the Major Arcana, and Ace, 2, and 3 of Cups in the Minor Arcana.

Lilith

Lilith is Earth's second satellite and has often been called the dark goddess. While her sister, the Moon, symbolizes traditionally accepted female roles, Lilith represents the darker side of femininity that people generally prefer not to speak about. Lilith has no time for emotional outbursts and can often seem cold and uncaring. She has no need of men, so is therefore often symbolized as a single or divorced woman. Although many do not attribute Lilith to any particular card, she should share rulership of The High Priestess with The Moon because she more closely identifies with the qualities represented in this card.

Mercury

Mercury is the closest planet to the Sun and has the fastest orbit of the nine known planets. Mercury is quick, witty, and communicative, is a fast learner and likes to teach what he knows to others. Because Mercury represents communication, intellect, and reason it can become critical, fussy, or overly concerned with detail. The negative aspect of Mercury is that it can gossip, lie, and slander if not well aspected in the natal horoscope. In astrology, Mercury rules Gemini and Virgo, and the third and sixth houses of the horoscope. In Tarot, Mercury rules The Magician in the Major Arcana.

Venus

Venus is known as the Morning or Evening Star because it is the last "star" to fade away when the sun brings the light of day and the first to be seen at dawn. Venus is charming, graceful, and diplomatic. Venus is very attractive and represents fertile womanhood, which indicates that men often cannot resist falling in love with her. She likes good food, drink, and sex, and may therefore have a tendency to overindulge. In astrology, Venus rules Taurus and Libra, and the second and seventh houses. In Tarot, Venus rules The Empress in the Major Arcana.

Mars

Mars is the red planet and its color signifies the energy it possesses. Mars can be aggressive; if its energy isn't controlled, accidents or mishaps may occur. It has a very adventurous spirit, which will prompt others to forge ahead when more timid souls would prefer to wait until better times appear. In ancient times Mars was considered to be a planet of fertility because much energy was needed to bring about the birth of a new plant, animal, or concept. In astrology, Mars rules Aries and the first house, and corules Scorpio and the eighth house. In Tarot, Mars rules The Tower in the Major Arcana.

Jupiter

Jupiter is the largest known planet in our solar system and represents expansion and growth. It brings luck, money, and abundance to whatever it comes in contact with. Jupiter is wise, understanding, and serves as the zodiacal mentor. In astrology, Jupiter rules Sagittarius and the ninth house, and corules Pisces and the twelfth house. In the Tarot, Jupiter rules the Wheel of Fortune in the Major Arcana.

Saturn

Saturn is such a majestic sight with its encircling rings, and this gas giant is oh-so-concerned about its reputation. Saturn is the taskmaster as it sets limitations and gives arduous lessons to be learned before the next step in the evolutionary process can be approached. Saturn is concerned with responsibility, duty, time, and age. Saturn can be a fearful sight to those who have not learned their lessons and taken obligations seriously. In astrology, Saturn rules Capricorn and the tenth house, and corules Aquarius and the eleventh house. In Tarot, Saturn rules The World in the Major Arcana.

Uranus

Uranus is such an oddball planet with its rings orbiting vertically rather than horizontally. This uniqueness pervades the planet that was rediscovered by an amateur astronomer instead of the traditional professionals of the day. With Uranus, only the unexpected can be expected. Uranus is the planet of change, genius, unconventional behavior, and revolution. In astrology, Uranus corules Aquarius and the eleventh house. In Tarot, Uranus rules The Fool in the Major Arcana, and 4, 5, and 6 of Swords in the Minor Arcana.

Neptune

Neptune is a watery, fluid planet whose gaseous fog and mist make it difficult for one to clearly see its surface. Neptune's fluid state makes it emotional, sensitive, intuitive, and psychic. Neptune can spend so much time daydreaming that it may not be in touch with reality, and is so vague that it can be quite deceptive. It seeks spirituality in the form of sacrifices, but is definitely not a pushover. This powerful planet wields a forceful energy that it can, and will, use to get its way in life. In astrology, Neptune corules Pisces and the twelfth house. In the Tarot, Neptune rules The Hanged Man in the Major Arcana, and 7, 8, and 9 of Cups in the Minor Arcana.

Pluto

Pluto is erratic and powerful. It is not a single, but actually a double planet with its relatively large moon orbiting in the same fashion as a double star. Pluto's orbit is not like the other planets because it is highly elliptical and it is at times the farthest-known planet in our solar system, but at others is inside Neptune's orbital path. While all of the other planets have a fairly even rate of travel throughout the twelve signs of the zodiac, Pluto's presence in a sign spans anywhere from fourteen years in Scorpio to thirty in Taurus. The more exploration that is done on this sometimes frozen, sometimes thawed planet can make one wonder just exactly which planet is actually the oddball of the solar system. Regardless of Pluto's eccentricities, it is very powerful indeed and has a tendency to destroy outmoded concepts in order to build anew. When Pluto makes an aspect during a transit, no one is left untouched from its influence. Pluto is lord of the underworld and is the planet of death and rebirth, symbolized by the fact that half of the time this planet is frozen and dead while the other half it is thawed and alive. In astrology, Pluto corules Scorpio and the eighth house. In the Tarot, Pluto rules Death in the Major Arcana.

North Node

The North Node of the Moon, or Dragon's Head, says "yes, yes, yes," and represents good fortune and luck that has been given to the native in this life to help him or her create their destiny. It is one of the things they are supposed to build upon and refine in this life. The North Node has many characteristics of Jupiter in that it is a free gift to the native. It should be noted, however, that many people must learn to act in accordance with the node because the concepts it brings are completely new and must be developed before they can come to fruition.

South Node

The South Node of the Moon, or the Dragon's Tail, says "no, no, no," and represents lessons, limitations, and restrictions. This is what the native has already developed in past lives and may have even abused. The South Node has many characteristics of Saturn in that it sometimes places harsh limitations on the areas of its concerns. It should be noted that because we have already developed the qualities and attributes of the South Node, it is all too compelling to slip back into its patterns whenever we are distressed or unsure of ourselves. Because it is our task to learn from mistakes, however, our higher selves will tend to put obstacles in our path that inhibit us from totally enmeshing ourselves in South Node areas.

Signs

The earth is the center of an imaginary circle called the zodiac. This zodiac is divided into twelve segments called signs, and each sign depicts certain traits. When all of the twelve characteristics are combined together they form the whole, or unity. The Sun, Moon, planets, and asteroids orbit the zodiac and are therefore posited in the various signs that help determine what influences will be present depending on the time and place. By casting a horoscope based on the exact time, date, and place of birth, much can be gleaned about the joys, happiness and successes, problems and lessons that will be prevalent during the life of the person or event.

Aries

Aries, the first sign of the zodiac, exemplifies its ambitious attitude by asserting it as the conqueror, emperor, warrior, or soldier of fortune. Aries is aggressive and forceful, and uses its energy to get what it desires. Aries has a great deal of enthusiasm for life and a sense of untamed daring, and early explorers of untamed wilderness have exemplified this sense of adventuresome. In astrology, Aries is ruled by the planet Mars and in turn rules the first house of the horoscope. In Tarot, Aries rules The Emperor in the Major Arcana and Ace, 2, and 3 of Wands in the Minor Arcana.

Taurus

Taurus, the second sign of the zodiac, comes into being when the farmers are tilling the fields and planting the crops. Taurus is fertile, voluptuous, sensual, practical, earthy, and materialistic. Taurus loves to be surrounded by luxury and is primarily concerned with accumulating wealth and prosperity. Don't be fooled by Taurus' sensual and pleasant nature because its stubbornness, combined with endurance and stamina, make it a formidable foe when its path has been crossed. In astrology, Taurus rules the second house of the horoscope and is ruled by Venus. In Tarot, Taurus rules The Hierophant in the Major Arcana, and 4, 5, and 6 of Pentacles in the Minor Arcana.

Gemini

Gemini, the third sign of the zodiac, comes into season as the weather warms up enough so people want to go places, visit friends, and socialize. Gemini is mental, active, and witty. It enjoys light, airy social contact, and is very communicative. Being the twins, Gemini often displays two personalities and can appear dualistic at times. Since Gemini has the gift of gab, it has been known to spread rumors and gossip if other stabilizing influences are not present. In astrology, Gemini rules the third house of the horoscope and is ruled by Mercury. In the Tarot, Gemini rules The Lovers in the Major Arcana, and 7, 8, and 9 of Swords in the Minor Arcana.

Cancer

Cancer, the fourth sign of the zodiac, is intuitive, sensitive, and emotional. The love Cancer sends out is pure and simple because she only wants to love, and in turn be loved. When confronted, Cancer normally reacts based upon emotions rather than intellect, and this can cause some difficulties if she is not able to control her behavior. Cancer is very protective of her home and family, and can consequently appear grasping and clinging if she feels she is not in control. In astrology, Cancer rules the fourth house of the horoscope and is ruled by the Moon. It should be noted that in ancient astrology the Moon was assigned rulership over only this sign while the other planets (with the exception of the Sun) were each allocated two signs to rule, one sign being active and the other inactive. This indicates that Cancer is a very powerful sign in its own right and encompasses both active and passive attributes. In the Tarot, Cancer rules The Chariot in the Major Arcana, and Ace, 2, and 3 of Cups in the Minor Arcana.

Leo

The Sun passes through Leo, the fifth sign of the zodiac, at the height of summer. People are laughing, singing, and enjoying themselves, and romance is in the air as lovers can be seen walking hand in hand throughout the long summer days. Likewise, children can be seen playing happily in the parks and streets during this carefree, enjoyable time. Resorts are full of vacationers who simply want to bask in the sun and enjoy their holiday. It should be noted that in ancient astrology the Sun was assigned rulership over only this sign where each planet (with the exception of the Moon) was allocated two signs to rule, one being active and the other passive. This indicates that Leo is a very powerful sign in its own right as it encompasses both active and passive genders. In astrology, Leo rules the fifth house of the horoscope and is ruled by the Sun. In the Tarot, Leo rules Strength in the Major Arcana, and 5, 6, and 7 of Wands in the Minor Arcana.

Virgo

After everyone has had their yearly dose of fun, Virgo, the sixth sign of the zodiac, calls people back to work as this is the month of harvest and preparation for the long winter ahead. Virgo goes about her duties in an efficient and unassuming manner, and can actually become embarrassed when others take notice of her accomplishments. She is concerned about health and hygiene, and is therefore likely to have a neat, clean house. In astrology, Virgo rules the sixth house of the horoscope, and is ruled by the planet Mercury. In the Tarot, Virgo rules The Hermit in the Major Arcana, and 7, 8, and 9 of Pentacles in the Minor Arcana.

Libra

Sooner or later people start thinking about making a permanent commitment to one another, and that's where Libra, the seventh sign of the zodiac, comes in. Libra is involved with all close relationships and partnerships. Because there is a fine line between love and hate, it should not be surprising to note that Libra also governs both close friendships and open enemies. Libra tries to be fair, but at times can appear judgmental. It tries to stay balanced, but only the weight of a feather gently placed on its scales can upset this complex harmony. In astrology, Libra rules the seventh house of the horoscope, and is ruled by the planet Venus. In the Tarot, Libra rules Justice in the Major Arcana, and Ace, 2, and 3 of Swords in the Minor Arcana.

Scorpio

Is it not surprising to find that after the crops have been harvested, the days have chilled, and people have returned to the warm confines of their homes, they finally have time to go deep within themselves and reflect upon their achievements and defeats. This is the effect that the eighth sign of the zodiac has on our deepest reflections. The emotions inherent in Scorpio are so extreme that compulsive or vindictive behavior is not uncommon. Scorpio's introspection allows people to honestly look within themselves, find out what needs to be transformed or healed, and emerge renewed and rejuvenated. Scorpio is good at keeping secrets. One of Scorpio's best-kept secrets is that death is but a veil that people must pass through so that they can be reborn anew into bodies stronger and wiser than before. In astrology, Scorpio rules the eighth house of the horoscope, and is coruled by Mars and Pluto. In the Tarot, Scorpio rules Judgement in the Major Arcana, and 4, 5, and 6 of Cups in the Minor Arcana.

Sagittarius

Such introspection and healing can leave a being quite somber and that's where Sagittarius, the ninth sign of zodiac, comes into play. Sagittarius' optimism and joviality make him the life of the party. Sagittarius also has a philosophical side as he seeks answers to religious, spiritual, or esoteric questions posed by philosophers throughout the ages. In his quest for knowledge, he has become wise and understanding, and is usually able to give sound advice when consulted. In astrology, Sagittarius rules the ninth house of the horoscope and is ruled by Jupiter. In the Tarot, Sagittarius rules Temperance in the Major Arcana, and 7, 8, and 9 of Wands in the Minor Arcana.

Capricorn

Capricorn, the tenth sign of the zodiac, instills responsibility, practicality, and discipline into our lives. Capricorn helps people become successful because it gives them a sense of purpose. Because Capricorn wants to be respected, it is very much concerned about its status and reputation in the community. Yes, it is true that Capricorn is materialistic and firmly grounded to the earth, but it does have a deeply hidden emotional side as well. It must be remembered that the symbol for Capricorn is a goat with a fish tail. People all too often play up the rugged image of the goat trying to climb up the mountain and quietly dismiss the fish tail that is earnestly swimming in a sea of emotion. Alas, poor Capricorn is often misunderstood and people sometimes fail to appreciate the much-needed grounding this sign provides. It should also be noted that ancient oriental drawings depict this sign placement as a fish or crab, so it may actually be that in the distant past this sign was in fact considered to be a water element. Therefore, the modern symbolism of a sea-goat may be an attempt to obtain symmetry between ancient emotional sensitivity and New Age practicality. In astrology, Capricorn rules the tenth house of the horoscope and is ruled by Saturn. In the Tarot, Capricorn rules The Devil in the Major Arcana, and 2, 3, and 4 of Pentacles in the Minor Arcana.

Aquarius

Aquarius, the eleventh sign of the zodiac, is intellectual, social, and thinks about future developments. In the symbology of this sign, the waterbearer is seen to be pouring a jug of fluid into a larger mass of water. The contents of the jug represent the knowledge he is carrying, and this act of pouring the liquid into a larger mass illustrates him disseminating knowledge to humanity. While Aquarius is friendly and sociable, it is also aloof, detached, and difficult to get close to, as evidenced by the fact that Aquarians as a rule have many acquaintances but few true friends. Aquarius dreams of a utopian society where there is no pain, suffering, or inequality. In astrology, Aquarius rules the eleventh house and is coruled Saturn and Uranus. In the Tarot, Aquarius rules The Star in the Major Arcana, and 4, 5, and 6 of Swords in the Minor Arcana.

Pisces

After people have been given the gift of knowledge, they soon begin to realize that the more they know, the more they don't know. At the vast immensity of this gulf of awareness, which is yet to be understood, they begin to ask spiritual questions such as:

- Who is responsible for the rules under which the universe was built?

- Is there more to reality than meets the eye?

- Why are these unfounded feelings so strong?

Pisces seeks to stretch beyond the reality of here and now, and search for clues to past, present, and future worlds, which is one of the reasons why Pisces normally responds to psychic impressions rather than cold, hard facts. In astrology, Pisces rules the twelfth house and is coruled by Jupiter and Neptune. In Tarot, Pisces is said to rule The Moon in the Major Arcana. More appropriately, Pisces is likely to corule The Moon and Lilith, the Earth's second esoteric satellite, and the 8, 9, and 10 of Cups in the Minor Arcana.

10

CABALA AND
THE TAROT

The Cabala is a system of Jewish mysticism that is thought to have originated in southern France and Spain in the twelfth and thirteenth centuries. The term "Cabala" was originally used to denote wisdom, inner knowledge, or understanding of the hidden mysteries, and it wasn't until much later that the term was used to refer to Jewish mysticism. The Cabala was intended to be a system of thought that allowed people to unravel the mysteries and unknown concepts concerning God and his or her creations.

Although this system of thought has historically been purported to be communicated by God to Adam, scholars tend to look for its origins in the first century before Christ.

The first document is considered to be the forerunner of Cabalism and the basis of the rest of it is the Sepher Yetzirah (Book of Formation), written by an anonymous author, most probably around the third century before Christ. The Sepher Yetzirah deals with the creation of the universe by means of the ten sephiram, which are archetypal numbers one through ten, and the twenty-two letters in the Hebrew alphabet.

Several versions of Cabala have evolved throughout the ages. The ancient Hebrew Cabala contained seven sephiram, which is reflected by the seven-pointed star (Star of David), the menorah, and the seven celestial bodies that were predominant influences prior to the discovery of the planets Uranus, Neptune, and Pluto. The ancient Iraqi Cabala had eight sephiram, which corresponds with the eight musical notes we use today. The modern Cabala, however, has ten primary sephiram, which corresponds with the decimal number system that is the foundation of today's economy. There are ten sephiram in the trestleboard that is used by most students of the Cabala today (see p. 150). An eleventh imaginary sephira, called Daath, is included in some versions of the Cabala, bringing the total number to eleven, a master number.

The Tree of Life, while not appearing until the Middle Ages, plays an important part in our philosophical systems of thought because it helps us to identify where we are in the grand scheme of things. The tree diagram is an important pictorial representation because it illustrates how the universe was created and is a map of the cosmos at all levels. A lightning flash is said to extend from the first sephira to the tenth—the lightning flash of creative energy proceeding from eternal unity. Ascending the tree describes the way back to unity, which instills in us knowledge and allows us to be reborn.

The Cabala is considered to be a separate branch of the esoteric studies, as is astrology, Tarot, and numerology. Many feel that the makers of the Tarot were at least familiar with the Cabala because of the intimate linking of the two sciences. Both the concepts are believed to have appeared in Europe at approximately the same period of time, with the Cabala possibly predating Tarot by about a hundred years. The Major Arcana in Tarot is composed of twenty-two cards, which is the number of letters in the Hebrew alphabet, the number of pathways in the Tree of Life trestleboard, and a master number in numerology. The ten numbered cards in each suit of the Minor Arcana correspond with the ten sephiram in the trestleboard. It is important to note that the trestleboard also appears on the Ten of Pentacles in the Rider-Waite deck, so Arthur Waite was at least familiar with the intricate interweavings between these two subjects when he designed his deck.

The Tree of Life consists of ten focal points, called *sephira*, and these ten sephiram are connected to twenty-two lines or pathways. These focal points are considered separate stages of God or aspects of life, and relate to the ten numbered cards in each suit of the Minor Arcana. The lines connecting the sephira correspond to the twenty-two letters in the Hebrew alphabet and the twenty-two cards in the Major Arcana.

Each sephira points to a specific character trait, which helps us to identify, exactly where we are in our evolutionary path to enlightenment. Each sephira in the trestleboard corresponds with a specific planet and is therefore closely aligned with the celestial art of astrology. The meanings of the ten sephiram, to include the eleventh imaginary one, are discussed on the following six pages.

Malkuth

Malkuth is position 10 of the Tree of Life and is associated with the keyword "Kingdom." It represents our roots, home, family, and close relationships. The essence of this sephira is the physical world and indicates what is presently manifest in our lives. This position represents our conscious awareness and the outcomes or results that we are now experiencing. Physically this node represents our physical body, musically it represents the musical note "do," and angelically it depicts the archangel Sandalphon. In astrology, the four elements fire, earth, air, and water rule this position. In Tarot, this position corresponds with the four cards numbered 10 in the Minor Arcana.

Yesod

Yesod is position 9 of the Tree of Life and is associated with the keyword "Foundation." This sephira denotes the collective unconscious or the vital soul of humanity. It gives insight into our life patterns because it shows our unconscious thoughts, secrets, hopes, desires, fears, and apprehensions. Yesod indicates whether our karmic lessons brought over from previous incarnations are beneficial, challenging, or debts we must repay. This focal point also indicates health matters, especially those that concern our overall well being. Physically this node represents our ego and angelically it depicts the archangel Gabriel. In astrology this position corresponds with the Moon, and in Tarot it relates to the four cards numbered 9 in the Minor Arcana.

Hod

Hod is position 8 of the Tree of Life and is associated with the keyword "Splendor." This sephira depicts worldly matters such as business, career, cultural, and artistic endeavors, and how these areas in our lives are being approached. It represents our analytical thought processes, our style of communication, and how we perceive our environment around us. Physically this node represents the theoretical aspects of life, musically it represents "ti," and angelically it depicts the archangel Michael. In astrology, the position corresponds with the planet Mercury, and in Tarot it denotes the four cards numbered 8 in the Minor Arcana.

Netzach

Netzach is in position 7 of the Tree of Life and is associated with the keyword "Victory." It represents our emotional attachments and feelings. This sephira tells us what we desire, what we are attracted to, and what type of people we form close relationships with. Physically this node represents the practical aspects of life, musically it represents "la," and angelically it depicts the archangel Haniel. In astrology, this position corresponds with the planet Venus, and in Tarot relates to the four cards numbered 7 in the Minor Arcana.

Tiphareth

Tiphareth is position 6 of the Tree of Life and is associated with the keyword "Beauty." It represents our higher self or true soul. It discusses the higher meaning of our lives and helps to define our life purposes, ideals, and objectives. This sephira depicts our achievements, successes, and the outer image we present to the world. This position is in the center of the trestleboard and represents the center of our being. In the physical world this node represents the self and angelically it depicts the archangel Raphael. In astrology, Tiphareth corresponds with the Sun, and in Tarot it relates to the four cards numbered 6 in the Minor Arcana.

Geburah

Geburah is position 5 of the Tree of Life and is associated with the keyword "Severity." It represents the conflicts and challenges we must overcome and the lessons we must learn. These lessons are generally seen as oppositions that we encounter, and which, unless appreciated for the strengthening qualities they impart, will tend to be seen as trials, tribulations, and limitations. This position also tells us the qualities we must utilize in order to effectively deal with difficulties. Utilizing the constructive influence of this position can help us to take greater responsibility for our lives, and make assets out of those areas that were once considered liabilities. Physically this node represents discipline, musically it represents "sol," and angelically it depicts the archangel Kamael. In astrology, this position corresponds with the planet Mars, and in Tarot it relates to the four cards numbered 5 in the Minor Arcana.

Chesed

Chesed is position 4 of the Tree of Life and is associated with the keyword "Mercy." It represents our opportunities for growth and rewards for the challenges we master. It indicates the most positive results we can gain from our thoughts, emotions, and actions, and shows us where we must exercise compassion. Chesed reflects the most positive aspects of all areas—even those areas that seem negative. This position provides us with a comfort zone in our lives because it gives us a sense of security. It also denotes our finances, wealth, and areas of abundance. Physically this node represents compassion, musically it represents "fa," and angelically it denotes the archangel Tzadqiel. In astrology, Chesed corresponds with the planet Jupiter, and in Tarot it relates to the four cards numbered 4 in the Minor Arcana.

Binah

Binah is position 3 of the Tree of Life and is associated with the keyword "Understanding." It is the feminine, right brain, or left side of ourselves, and represents inner knowledge or the divine mother within us. Binah often depicts our intuitive processes and what areas we are receptive to. This position shows what experiences we have chosen to bring to experience through the process of manifestation and denotes those areas that tend to be limiting or containing, thus helping to give us greater understanding and depth through dealing constructively with these difficulties. Physically this node represents reason, musically it represents the note "mi," and angelically it depicts the archangel Tzaphqiel. In astrology, this position corresponds with the planet Saturn, and in Tarot it corresponds with the four cards numbered 3 in the Minor Arcana.

Chokmah

Chokmah is position 2 of the Tree of Life and is associated with the keyword "Wisdom." It is associated with the masculine, right side of ourselves and is sometimes depicted as the cosmic father within us. Chokmah represents our learned behavior and actions and shows where our responsibilities lie. It indicates our ability to use rationale and logic to make choices and decisions. Physically this node represents revelation, musically it depicts the note "re," and angelically it depicts the archangel Raziel. In astrology, the position corresponds with Uranus, and in Tarot it relates to the four cards numbered 2 in the Minor Arcana.

Kether

Kether is position 1 of the Tree of Life and is associated with the keyword "Crown." It represents our creative potentials and new beginnings. Kether depicts our spiritual world, religious attitudes, and general inner state of being. This sephira is considered the indivisible one and is therefore complete in itself. It shows what we have chosen to manifest and what we desire to accomplish through our life experiences. Musically this node represents the note "do," and angelically it depicts the archangel Metatron. In astrology, the position corresponds with Uranus, and in the Tarot, this position denotes cards numbered 1 in the Minor Arcana.

Daath

Daath is an invisible sephira between Tiphareth and Kether. It is an interfacing node, which gives the entire Tree of Life a sense of completion. It represents the powerful knowledge that we have within ourselves, and astrologically it is ruled by the planet Pluto.

The 22 Pathways

0. The Fool

Pathway 0 connects sephira Kether with Chokmah. The energy of The Fool combines wisdom with creativity to provide new beginnings, unconditional love, and sometimes even a choice that needs to be made in this life.

1. The Magician

Pathway 1 connects sephira Kether with Binah. The energy of The Magician combines understanding with creativity to give us the tools necessary to manifest and create our own reality. The use of words is of great importance and it must be emphasized that any correspondence should be entered into ethically, otherwise dubious liaisons could be formed that will inhibit soul growth.

2. The High Priestess

Pathway 2 connects sephira Kether with Tiphareth. The energy of The High Priestess combines the creative flow with beauty to provide us with the secrets of the universe. These principles are available to us all, but some have chosen to suppress this knowledge because of the particular life into which they have incarnated.

3. The Empress

Pathway 3 connects sephira Binah with Chokmah. The energy of The Empress combines understanding with wisdom to provide the ultimate feminine energy. In Western society we tend to promote more aggressive, outgoing masculine character traits, and downplay intuitive qualities. However, in

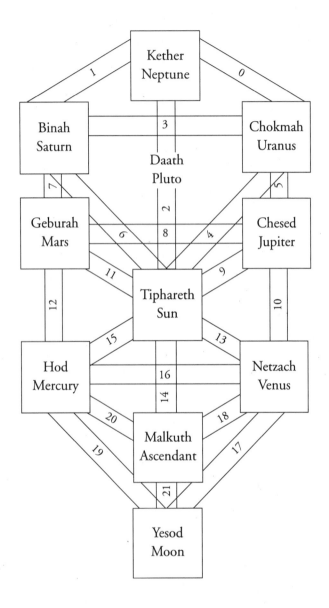

The Tree of Life Trestleboard

order to become whole we must balance our feminine and masculine sides to more fully honor both aspects of our being. Only when our male and female halves have reached equilibrium will we be capable of reaching our highest potential.

4. The Emperor

Pathway 4 connects sephira Chokmah with Tiphareth. The energy of The Emperor combines wisdom with beauty to provide the masculine character. Although The Emperor rules authoritatively, he possesses the necessary wisdom to make sound decisions and an inherent sense of grace to enable him to communicate tactfully to those in a subordinate position.

5. The Hierophant

Pathway 5 connects sephira Chokmah and Chesed. The energy of The Hierophant combines wisdom with mercy to provide the traditional pathway to religion via churches and other similar institutions. This pathway enables us to come to God via the more traditional route of a priest or holy person who intercedes for us because we are not yet ready to approach God ourselves. Although we inherently possess everything we need to achieve oneness with God, we sometimes prefer to give our power over to an intermediary because then we are able to hand over responsibility for our actions to that person. This intermediary is often typified by the priest in the church who presides over religious ceremonies and acts as the confessor in his community.

6. The Lovers

Pathway 6 connects sephira Binah with Tiphareth. The energy of The Lovers combines understanding with beauty to enable us to have satisfying relationships. The Lovers signify the type of love that is typical of soulmate and eternal lovemate relationships. In addition to developing meaningful relationships with others, The Lovers also help us to be true, honest, and happy with ourselves.

7. The Chariot

Pathway 7 connects sephira Binah with Geburah. The energy of The Chariot combines understanding with severity to help us achieve victory in our lives. The Chariot is persistent and never accepts defeat, and therefore will ultimately succeed, even under the most trying of circumstances.

8. Strength

Pathway 8 connects sephira Geburah to Chesed. The energy of Strength overcomes severity and uses mercy to become strong and enduring. This strength tends to come from within and is usually brought about through harsh circumstances, which enables us to become more merciful when confronted with the problems of others.

9. The Hermit

Pathway 9 connects sephira Chesed and Tiphareth. The energy of The Hermit combines mercy and beauty to achieve an inner awareness that comes about only through meditation and quiet time alone.

10. Wheel of Fortune

Pathway 10 connects sephira Chesed with Netzach. The energy of Wheel of Fortune combines Mercy with Victory to bring about a change in circumstances, which will ultimately yield good fortune.

11. Justice

Pathway 11 connects sephira Geburah with Tiphareth. The energy of Justice combines severity with beauty to put balance in our lives. The term "poetic justice" is an appropriate phrase that aptly describes this pathway. Whether in this life or the next, we must be held accountable for and face our past actions in a just manner if we hope to evolve into the next level of awareness.

12. The Hanged Man

Pathway 12 connects sephira Geburah with Hod. The energy of The Hanged Man combines severity and splendor to provide spiritual awareness. This cosmic knowledge usually comes at a price, as a sacrifice may be necessary to achieve it.

13. Death

Pathway 13 connects sephira Tiphareth with Netzach. The energy of the angel of Death combines beauty and victory to transcend physical boundaries and emerge reborn. Death indicates a major change about to occur in our lives, which may require an outmoded concept to be discarded for a newer, better one.

14. Temperance

Pathway 14 connects sephira Tiphareth with Yesod. The energy of the angel of Temperance combines beauty with foundation to provide temperance and balance in lifestyle. With temperance, an attitude of moderation in all things is necessary, because life seems to run more smoothly when this is achieved.

15. The Devil

Pathway 15 connects sephira Tiphareth with Hod. The energy of The Devil, which isn't really evil in itself, combines beauty with splendor to achieve materialism in the form of wealth. Many people believe The Devil is wicked, which is a depiction that is not necessarily true. The Devil merely represents the more physical, materialistic urges of our being and this drive for earthly pleasures helps us create the splendor, beauty, and wealth that we desire.

16. The Tower

Pathway 16 connects sephira Hod with Netzach. The energy of The Tower combines splendor and victory to bring about radical upheavals. These upheavals are generally caused by a false sense of security. The Tower presses us to action so we can change our circumstances. These disturbances will ultimately turn out for the best, but we may beg to differ when the cataclysms are occurring because, when it is all over, our lifestyle will have dramatically changed.

17. The Star

Pathway 17 connects sephira Netzach with Yesod. The energy of The Star combines victory with foundation to bring about intellectual awareness and enlightenment. The Star distributes knowledge to all of humanity to awaken them to universal truths and concepts because when possessed with factual information, we are better able to decide which spiritual path we would like to pursue.

18. The Moon

Pathway 18 connects sephira Netzach with Malkuth. The energy of The Moon combines victory with the kingdom of God to produce intuition and a more feminine aspect of the universal oneness. The perceptive, intuitive attributes of the nebulous Moon add vague, mysterious elements to the God-force. Archaeological findings clearly suggest that ancient religions predating Abraham were predominantly matrilineal—most probably because females are capable of giving birth while men are not. Unfortunately, since the time of Abraham, God was seen as wholly masculine, due to invading patrilineal tribes from the north. Perhaps in time the concept of God will evolve to integrate both masculine and feminine qualities so men and women alike will be able to appreciate its essence.

19. The Sun

Pathway 19 connects sephira Hod with Yesod. The energy of The Sun combines splendor with foundation to provide happiness and exuberance. The Sun gives us the love of life to help us to build upon the foundation of our reality. It also provides us with an awareness and insight into the agendas of those around us to help us make important decisions with regard to how we would like to live our lives.

20. Judgement

Pathway 20 connects sephira Hod with Malkuth. The energy of Judgement combines splendor with the kingdom of God to allow us to emerge reborn. If we have led righteous lives, our judgment will therefore reflect the rewards of our lifestyle. However, if we have committed wrongs then we will be required to eventually atone for those errs in this or subsequent incarnations. Judgments can be rather extreme during the healing process and we may wonder if we are in fact being restored to a perfected state because of the inherent pain we endure during the purifying process. We will, however, emerge reborn, if not a little wiser for the tests we have encountered.

21. The World

Pathway 21 connects sephira Yesod with Malkuth. The energy of The World combines the earthly foundation with the kingdom of God to complete the cycle of our terrestrial existence. Upon completion of this cycle, we will begin new tasks that will also need to be seen through to completion.

11

I CHING AND
THE TAROT

While the Western world uses Tarot and its derivative oracles to delve into the subtle influences of the psyche, the eastern hemisphere has traditionally used the I Ching, or Book or Changes, when pondering the best course of action to take in certain situations.

The authorship of the I Ching is unknown, but it is possibly the oldest written work in the world. As oral parables, the I Ching were handed down from generation to generation for not less than 3,000 years. These philosophies and laws of transformation illustrating the cycles of existence that humans normally encounter during their lives were recorded in book form about 3,000 years ago.

While the occidental world has viewed any intuitive tool with attitudes ranging from humorous disbelief to derisive contempt, the oriental viewpoint is much different. Eastern countries such as China, Japan, Korea, and Vietnam have relied upon the Book of Changes from remote antiquity until the present to help them make decisions. Confucius is said to have relied heavily upon the I Ching in developing the code of living named for him. The samurai used the I Ching to form one of the best fighting forces in the world, and the Japanese owed much of their early military victories to the guidance provided in this oracle.

While the I Ching is considered to be fluid and changing, giving advice in very much the same way as a wise friend would, there are many close correlations between the I Ching and Tarot. The Tarot utilizes seventy-eight cards that describe the different facets of a person's life, and the I Ching contains sixty-four primary parables that detail the various stages of transformation through the cycle of life. Both the I Ching and Tarot's divination principles are based upon the theory of synchronicity, or an incredible coincidence that enables them to provide reliable and accurate readings. Additionally, both oracles can help us delve into the more subtle nuances of human behavior and interaction.

There are several ways to consult the Book of Changes. The traditional oriental method is to utilize an elaborate method of throwing yarrow sticks—the way the sticks fall determine the answer. Another method of divination is to toss three coins to obtain an appropriate answer. I Ching cards, which can be used by randomly drawing a card, have been developed for those who feel more comfortable with such a system. Some students of the I Ching have dispensed with the yarrow sticks, coins, and cards altogether, and simply open the book to a random page. The answer to the question will be found within the text.

When consulting the I Ching, the querent may sometimes receive an answer, which seems to have no correlation to the question asked. In instances like this, his or her higher self may be trying to bring to light a situation that needs attention. For this reason any response, regardless of how absurd it seems, needs to be given careful consideration.

Each parable of the I Ching corresponds to a specific card in the Tarot, enabling greater understanding of both oracles if they are used interchangeably and studied for greater clarity.

Tarot Correspondences with the I Ching

1	Creative Power	Ace of Swords/Knight of Swords
2	Natural Response	The Empress
3	Difficult Beginnings	Ace of Wands
4	Inexperience	The Fool
5	Waiting Nourishment	Four of Cups
6	Conflict	Seven of Swords
7	Collective Force	Judgement
8	Unity	The Lovers
9	Restrained	King of Swords/Knight of Swords
10	Correctness	Page of Swords
11	Prosperity	Strength
12	Stagnation	Death/Five of Pentacles
13	Community	Two of Wands
14	Sovereignty	Six of Wands
15	Moderation	Temperance
16	Enthusiasm	Three of Pentacles/Knight of Cups
17	Adapting	Eight of Cups
18	Repair	The Hierophant
19	Promotion	Ace of Pentacles/Knight Pentacles

20	Contemplation	Queen of Swords
21	Reform	Five of Wands
22	Grace	Eight of Pentacles
23	Deterioration	The Tower
24	Repeating	Wheel of Fortune
25	Innocence	Page of Pentacles
26	Grounding	The Hermit
27	Nourishing	Six of Pentacles
28	Excess	The Emperor
29	Danger	The High Priestess
30	Caressing Fire	The Sun
31	Attraction	Two of Cups
32	Duration	The Chariot
33	Withdrawal	Four of Swords
34	Great Power	King of Wands
35	Progress	The Magician/Three of Wands
36	Censorship	Nine of Wands/Five of Swords
37	Family	The World/Six of Cups
38	Contradiction	Seven of Wands
39	Obstacles	Seven of Pentacles
40	Liberation	Ten of Cups
41	Decline	Page of Cups
42	Benefit	Three of Swords
43	Resolution	Page of Wands
44	Temptation	Six of Swords/Devil
45	Assembling	Ten of Pentacles/Four of Pentacles
46	Advancement	Queen of Pentacles
47	Weariness	Five of Cups/Eight of Cups
48	The Well	Nine of Cups

49	Changing	The Hanged Man
50	Cosmic Order	King of Cups
51	Awakening	Four of Wands
52	Meditation	Nine of Pentacles
53	Developing	King of Pentacles
54	Living Together	Three of Cups
55	Zenith	Justice/Nine of Cups
56	Traveling	Eight of Wands
57	Willing Submission	Two of Swords
58	Joy	Ace of Cups
59	Dispersion	Ten of Swords
60	Limitations	Seven of Cups/Two of Pentacles
61	Inner Truth	Queen of Cups
62	Continuing	Queen of Wands
63	Completions	The Moon
64	Beginnings	The Star

The Major Arcana

The Fool	4	Innocence
The Magician	35	Success
The High Priestess	29	Danger
The Empress	2	Natural Response
The Emperor	28	Excess
The Hierophant	18	Decay
The Lovers	8	Unity
The Chariot	32	Duration
Strength	11	Prosperity
The Hermit	26	Grounding

The Suit of Wands

The Suit of Pentacles

Ace	19	Promotion
Two	60	Limitations
Three	16	Enthusiasm
Four	45	Assembling
Five	12	Stagnation
Six	27	Nourishing
Seven	39	Obstacles
Eight	22	Grace
Nine	52	Meditation
Ten	45	Assembling
Page	25	Innocence
Knight	19	Promotion
Queen	46	Advancement
King	53	Developing

The Suit of Swords

Ace	1	Creative Power
Two	57	Willing Submission
Three	42	Benefit
Four	33	Withdrawal
Five	36	Censorship
Six	44	Temptation
Seven	6	Collective Force
Eight	47	Weariness
Nine	9	Restrained
Ten	59	Dispersion
Page	10	Correctness
Knight	1	Creative Power

12

RUNES AND
THE TAROT

Runes (translated as "a secret thing, a mystery") are a sacred alphabet used as late as the Middle Ages by the Scandinavians. The secret language of the runes was passed down through the generations from master to apprentice via legomonism, or sacred initiations, and their messages were therefore never recorded. For this reason, the wisdom that the runic masters possessed died with them, leaving nothing but the remnants of sagas, or runic lore, and the runes themselves.

Because the runes are an ancient divinatory device predating Christianity's New Testament, they bring into our consciousness a more grounded, earthy value system that portrays their development.

Runes, basically stones with pictorial symbols inscribed on them, are drawn at random to answer specific questions. Like the Tarot, they should not be used too often. The first answer is correct, and repetitive queries regarding the same issue will merely yield misleading results. Because runes and Tarot are both divinatory devices, based on Jung's theory of synchronicity, or meaningful coincidence, they can be linked in meaning to give further clarification in a reading. Correlations are listed below:

Rune and Significance			**Tarot Correspondence**	
1	Mannaz	The Self	4	The Emperor
2	Gebo	Partnership	6	The Lovers
3	Ansuz	Signals	1	The Magician
4	Othila	Separation	5	The Hierophant
5	Uruz	Strength	8	Strength
6	Perth	Initiation	2	The High Priestess
7	Nauthiz	Constraint	14	Temperance
8	Inguz	Fertility	3	The Empress
9	Eihwaz	Defense	9	of Wands
10	Algiz	Protection	18	The Moon
11	Fehu	Possessions	15	The Devil
12	Wunjo	Joy	17	The Star
13	Jera	Harvest	9	The Hermit
14	Kano	Opening	19	The Sun
15	Teiwaz	Victory	10	Wheel of Fortune
16	Berkana	Rebirth	20	Judgement
17	Ehwaz	Movement	7	Chariot
18	Laguz	Flow		Ace from any suit
19	Hagalaz	Disruptive Forces	16	Tower
20	Raido	A Journey	8	of Wands
21	Thurisaz	Gateway	11	Justice
22	Dagaz	Breakthrough	13	Death
23	Isa	Standstill	12	The Hanged Man
24	Sowelu	Wholeness	21	The World
25	Odin	The Unknowable	0	The Fool

13

COLOR AND
THE TAROT

Color is an integral part of our existence. Everywhere we look we find it—in our clothing, furnishings, natural settings, and even our personalities. Color is revealed in our daily speech in terms such as "a blue mood," "green with envy," "he saw red," or the calling of a person "yellow" to imply that he is cowardly in some way. The world would be a pretty drab place if we only perceived varying shades of black, white, and gray—it would be a monochromatic view. From an exoteric perspective, color is actually a vibration of light and what we see is a reflection of that essence, revealed in a wide variety of hues that can add flavor to our visual perceptions. We can perceive the shades of color reflected through the rainbow or nature's prism, as well as in the energy field that envelopes our bodies. Even those who are visually impaired are able to perceive the vibratory rate of colors, whether in their mind's eye or through the sense of feel, sound, or smell.

The psychological preference for certain colors is evidenced by the traditional meanings we associate with the shades, such as when brides wear white, mourners wear black, and authority figures wear blue or black. The reasons we subconsciously select one color over another may have psychological implications that transcend conscious awareness, because color carries archetypal elements dating back to antiquity. Therefore, since Tarot is comprised of seventy-eight pictographs, which include color as a means to convey their message, it is important to develop an awareness of the power this perception wields in order to more accurately interpret the cards.

Red

Red is the first color in the light spectrum that can be seen by the human eye. It is representative of survival instincts, action, and security. As a rule, red represents our sex drive because it governs the sexual organs. A lesser-known fact about this color is that it actually rules a person's ability to feel secure with himself and is associated with the base of the spine. Because red has so much energy that it possesses the will to succeed it is associated with 7, Chariot. When used negatively, such as when too much aggression or rash behavior is evident, complications can occur and it is in these occasion when 16, The Tower is employed.

Orange

Orange is the second color to be seen in the spectrum and represents liveliness and happy memories. Because of its vibrancy, many young people are drawn to the warming influence it projects. Orange governs the kidneys and brings about an emotional release of energy by those who wear it. Because orange deals with our ability to procreate, the fertility of 3, The Empress is involved, influenced by the vibrancy of orange.

Yellow

Yellow is considered to represent the intellect because it is associated with mental imagery. It governs the solar plexus and, like the Sun, is a vibrant life force. It is happy, lively, and promotes a sense of self-confidence to help us cope during stressful situations. 19, The Sun, which encompasses its love of life, is representative of this color.

Green

Although when jealous one is said to be "green with envy," this color is actually a hue used principally for healing because its calming, soothing properties help to promote health and well-being. Green governs the heart and is therefore associated with love and harmony. Because we strive to maintain equilibrium even under the most extreme of circumstances, 14, Temperance influences this color.

Pink

Pink is a color of love, compassion and femininity. It cogoverns the heart with green and represents understanding and admiration. Pink is often associated with happy memories because it brings us in touch with good times of long ago. An element of love would be involved in any emotional endeavor, so 6, The Lovers is representative of this color.

Turquoise

Turquoise is a color of deep compassion and inner healing, and relates to our ability to love ourselves as well as others. Turquoise governs the thymus and is therefore related to the immune system of the body. When we love unconditionally we often must love those whose lifestyles are completely different from our own. For this reason we must let go of pre-conceived notions if we are to grow and develop on our path to becoming celestial beings. 12, The Hanged Man is an apt archetype to govern turquoise. As we learn to love those who do not necessarily live their lives the way that we would prefer, we will ultimately gain much knowledge of others as well as ourselves. For this reason 2, The High Priestess, and 5, The Hierophant represent turquoise.

Blue

Blue is universally considered to be the friendliest color in the spectrum and people who wear this shade are seen as approachable and socially aware. Because blue governs the throat, it corresponds with our ability to communicate with others. When we have colds and sore throats this may be an indication that we need to be more conscientious about how we relate to others. Because blue is so amiable and eager to express itself, 1, The Magician carries with it the tones of this color.

Purple

Purple has long been considered the color of royalty, dating back to a time when the monarchy was thought to have a direct link to God. Purple is associated with the brow, or third eye, and represents insight, wisdom, and our ability to see beyond what is considered the normal span of visual perception. The archetype of 4, The Emperor carries with it the universal influences of purple. This is a useful card to reflect on when important life decisions need to be made.

Magenta

Magenta is a mixture of red and purple, and is considered to represent universal harmony. It governs the crown of the head and deals with our ability to transcend the here and now to experience a sense of higher cognition. This color is strong, bright, and carries with it a sense of vivacity. Because we all actually possess the ability to tap into the universal store of knowledge, 9, The Hermit helps us to find the answers to the probing questions within ourselves.

Indigo

Indigo is a mixture of blue and purple, and contains much depth, dating back to the attire of early spiritual leaders. Because this color is associated with the crown, it is considered to be one of the most inspired colors in the spectrum. When we are attuned to our crown chakra we will ultimately possess the knowledge that we need to progress along our path. It is for this reason that there will be occasions when we will live under the vibrational influences of 21, The World and conclude a part of our lives, or simulate the activities of 0, The Fool and begin an entirely new venture.

Lavender

Lavender is a calming color that is approachable and puts others at ease. When we are tense due to the stressors in our lives it is useful to meditate on 8, Strength to help maintain harmony during difficult times.

White

White is a combination of all the colors within the light spectrum. It is considered to be a color of truth, knowledge, and illumination. 17, The Star is representative of the infinite knowledge that flows through white. White embodies clarity and understanding, which will ultimately bring good fortune as we attune to its universal harmony, so 10, Wheel of Fortune is indicative of this color.

Brown

Brown is a combination of the three primary colors: red, yellow, and blue. It is an earthy, practical color that is sincere in nature but may be considered to be a bit too conventional for some. Because 15, The Devil is concerned with the earthly events of here and now, its most positive aspects are reflected in this color.

Black

Black is considered to be the absence of color and is often misunderstood. On many occasions this hue represents unresolved, thwarted ambitions that have resulted in disease, and at other times it symbolizes a profound forgetfulness, as in cases when people lose sight of their purpose in life. Although this color has been given much bad publicity throughout the ages, deep velvety black can actually bring about an intense sense of healing that cannot be penetrated by the other colors and it is for this reason that many people in mourning choose to wear it. 13, Death represents this color's apocalyptic nature, while 20, Judgement calls into play the deep inner healing that is necessary to transform our being. 18, The Moon disables our ability to clearly remember all that has been and all that ever will be so that we can evolve ourselves without outside intervention.

Gray

Gray is a combination of white and black, and has the unusual distinction of being a combination of all colors and absence of color at the same time. Gray indicates that balance must be achieved when two opposing viewpoints are at play to influence an outcome either positively or negatively. It is for this reason that 11, Justice vibrates the essence of gray.

14

CHAKRAS AND
THE TAROT

Chakras are wheels of energy running throughout the body to help our body, mind, and soul function properly. Some people are actually able to see the color, shape, and direction the chakra is turning in the body and are able to analyze any problem areas the person may be experiencing merely by observing them. There are hundreds of chakras in the body and some ancient Indian and Tibetan texts actually speak of 350,000 *nadis*, or minor chakras running throughout the body. Of these hundreds of chakras, there are seven major and twenty-one minor points of energy.

It is well known that our minds are integrally connected to our bodies, because a large proportion of illnesses are actually due to psychosomatic responses or stressors that we are not able to resolve in our daily lives. The chakras correspond to specific aspects of how our body, mind, and spirit are working together to form our whole being. If one chakra is blocked or not working properly because of any type of emotional, physical, or mental stress, we may suffer some physical discomfort associated with that area. If the stress is not relieved, or the problem not resolved, we might eventually develop a disease that manifests itself in our bodies. For this reason it is very important that our chakras are regularly aligned and corrected to stay healthy in body, mind, and spirit.

Locating the Chakras

There are many different theories of where the chakras actually are and their importance in our lives, but the ten points discussed in the following paragraphs are common among most schools of thought.

Root Chakra

The root chakra, or kundalini, is located at the base of the spine. This chakra is associated with the color red and is represented by a snake. The sleeping snake is coiled up at the base of the spine, and, upon awakening, like a cobra it shoots up through all the chakras to the crown. The root chakra is the seat of the physical body and is responsible for our spatial intuition or ability to perceive space and time. The root serves to keep us in our bodies, grounded to the earth, and governs our vitality, energy, gut instincts, and survival mechanisms. The root chakra governs issues relating to the material world, success, stability, security, courage, and patience. When we are negatively relating to root chakra issues, we may be self-centered, insecure, violent, greedy, and angry. Physically, the root chakra governs the colon, adrenal glands, kidneys, spinal column, legs, and bones. If we have long-standing negative issues relating to the root chakra that have not been resolved, we may soon begin to manifest symptoms

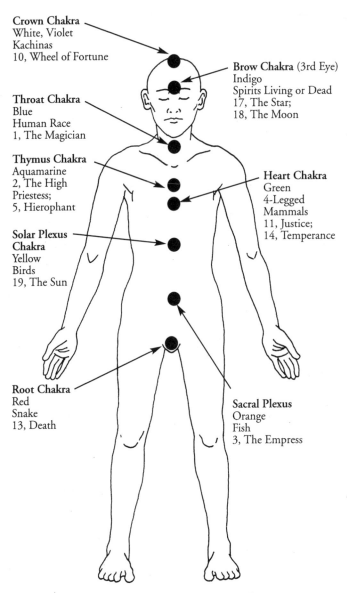

Crown Chakra
White, Violet
Kachinas
10, Wheel of Fortune

Brow Chakra (3rd Eye)
Indigo
Spirits Living or Dead
17, The Star;
18, The Moon

Throat Chakra
Blue
Human Race
1, The Magician

Thymus Chakra
Aquamarine
2, The High
Priestess;
5, Hierophant

Heart Chakra
Green
4-Legged
Mammals
11, Justice;
14, Temperance

**Solar Plexus
Chakra**
Yellow
Birds
19, The Sun

Root Chakra
Red
Snake
13, Death

Sacral Plexus
Orange
Fish
3, The Empress

The Chakras and Their Correspondences

of the problem in our physical bodies. These physical symptoms will likely become apparent in elimination problems such as constipation, diarrhea, kidney stones, renal colic, bone disease, or spinal problems. People who tend to activate our root chakra are our parents and grandparents, people who influence our security, and people with whom we have traditional relationships. Because this chakra deals with our innermost level of being, it corresponds with the two transcendental qualities of 13, Death. Because our ability to feel secure means that we sometimes defer to others, 4, The Emperor is a representative symbol. During those times when our security is at risk, such as the threat of losing our jobs, homes, wealth, or even someone we love, we will no doubt do whatever is necessary to retain what we are in fear of losing. It is for this reason 7, The Chariot is a suitable card to reflect on. There will be occasions when we need to be shaken out of our complacency, and 16, The Tower is the focal operative in such situations.

Sacral Plexus

The sacral plexus, or sexual chakra, is located in the lower abdomen, about two inches below the navel. This chakra is associated with the color orange and is represented by a fish. Since the sacral plexus is the seat of the emotional body, watery, aquatic animals are appropriate beings to represent this chakra. The sacral plexus governs our ability to receive feelings or sensations from beings beyond time and space, and governs our ability to feel and release our emotions. The sacral plexus governs issues relating to our sexuality and sensuality, physical force and vitality, giving and receiving of emotions, desire, pleasure, sexual and passionate love, change, movement, assimilation of new ideas, health, tolerance, surrender, and working harmoniously with others.

When we are negatively relating to the sacral plexus, we may overindulge in food, sex, or drugs, experience sexual difficulties, feel confused, feel a sense of purposeless in life, experience feelings of jealousy or envy, or desire to possess people or material wealth. Physically, the sacral plexus governs the reproductive organs, spleen and bladder. If we have long-standing negative issues relating to the sacral chakra that have not been resolved or healed, we may eventually become physically ill. These physical ailments can include sexual difficulties such as impotence or frigidity, bladder infections, and problems with the reproductive organs including cysts, fibroids, and sexually transmitted diseases. People who activate our sacral plexus are our lovers and people we tend to react to emotionally.

Because the sacral plexus governs fertility on either a physical or emotional level, the archetype of 3, The Empress invariably emanates from this point. When we are positively expressing our sexuality, which comes about from the love we give to another person, then 6, The Lovers is an appropriate card. If, however, we use our sexuality in a negative way, such as in the pursuit of power or wealth, then 15, The Devil is an accurate representation of this chakra.

Solar Plexus

The solar plexus is located above the navel and below the chest. This chakra is associated with the color yellow. Since the solar plexus is the seat of the mental body, which is represented by the element air, birds are considered to be appropriate significators because they fly in the sky. The solar plexus is also symbolized by the sun because this chakra brings the life force to us. This chakra enables us to pick up vibrations and essences from people, places, and things. The solar plexus vitalizes the sympathetic nervous system associated with stressful situations, the digestive process, metabolism and emotions, and controls the functioning of the pancreas, adrenal glands, stomach, liver, gallbladder, nervous system, and muscles. This chakra governs issues relating to will, personal power, authority, energy, mastery of desire, and self-control.

When we are positively reacting to situations relating to the solar plexus, we will generally experience a lot of radiance, warmth, a sense of awakening and transformation, and happiness. When we take on more responsibility than we can effectively deal with or put too much emphasis on power or authority, we may find that we are negatively reacting to solar plexus issues. These stressors may in turn cause us to experience anger, fear, or even hate. If we have long-standing unresolved problems relating to the solar plexus, they may begin to manifest themselves in our physical bodies to force us to confront the problem. These symptoms will likely exhibit themselves in the form of digestive problems such as ulcers, liver, or pancreas problems.

People who activate our solar plexus are friends, classmates, intellectuals, politicians, coworkers, or supervisors. Because the solar plexus is indicative of our ability to give and receive love, then 19, The Sun is representative of this point. When we are feeling under the weather, however, we should align ourselves with 8, Strength to help us persevere, even under the most trying of circumstances.

Heart Chakra

The heart chakra is located in the center of the chest. This chakra is associated with the color green and all four-legged mammals. The heart chakra is the seat of the astral body, which is the bridge between the material and spiritual bodies. This chakra deals with empathy or our ability to imaginatively project a subjective thought into an object so that the object appears to be infused with the thought. The heart chakra energizes our physical bodies with the life force and helps ground the energy to our bodies. This chakra governs issues relating to unconditional love, feelings, forgiveness, compassion, understanding, openness, balance, trust, and oneness with life. When we negatively relate to heart chakra issues, we may repress love and become unbalanced, distrustful, and emotionally unstable.

Physically, the heart chakra governs the circulation of blood, heart, arms, hands, and lungs. When we have long-standing emotional problems relating to the heart chakra, we may develop heart problems, lung disease, or circulation problems, in order to force us to come to terms with these issues. People who tend to activate our heart chakra are those who teach us to love unconditionally, and these persons may put us into positions where we are forced to love them regardless of their wrongdoings. Because the heart chakra helps us remain balanced throughout life's ups and downs, the harmonious qualities of 11, Justice and 14, Temperance represent this chakra. Because we are often asked to love unconditionally those who at seem to act at cross-purposes to our lives, 12, The Hanged Man asks us to make such sacrifices—as all that we give will eventually come back to us stronger than ever before.

Thymus Chakra

The thymus is a secondary chakra located just above the heart chakra. Some feel that in this new age of spiritual awakening, the thymus is taking on greater importance as a major chakra. This chakra is associated with the color aquamarine, and has a large influence on our telepathy. It is a gland located just above the heart and works primarily in babies and young children to develop their immune system. By the age of about ten it has already begun to atrophy and until recently was considered to be of no use to the adult human. The thymus chakra governs our ability to be at peace with ourselves, to feel compassion for others, be connected with humanity, and feel unconditional love for others. When we are negatively relating to thymus chakra issues, we may find ourselves becoming judgmental, self-righteous, and uncompassionate. We may also feel we are unworthy to continue in the human race. When we are not relating properly to thymus chakra issues, our body's immune system may weaken so that we are more susceptible to colds and other viruses. If after an extended period of time we are still not able to resolve thymus chakra issues, our immune system may totally break down, exposing us to life-threatening ailments. People who activate our thymus chakra are those who force us to feel compassion or empathy, and those who teach us unconditional love. Because the thymus chakra asks us to look within and love aspects of ourselves or others, 2, The High Priestess and 5, Hierophant are called into play to help us to discover the more esoteric elements of our existence.

Throat Chakra

The throat chakra is located in the region of the throat. This chakra is associated with the color blue and represents the human race. The throat chakra is the seat of the etheric body, the hologram of our life, and is responsible for clairaudience, or our ability to hear beyond the normal hearing range. The throat chakra governs our ability to communicate with one another, self-expression, the spoken word, creative expression, truth, knowledge, wisdom, honesty, and reliability. When we are not in touch with the issues that relate to our throat chakra we may begin to have speech difficulties, use our knowledge unwisely, tell untruths, use the spoken or written word to manipulate or control, or lack ability to accurately discern life situations.

Physically, the throat chakra governs the thyroid glands, throat, and mouth. If we continue to relate to these concerns in a negative manner over an extended period of time, we may eventually become depressed, have thyroid problems, and develop sore throats, cold sores, and earaches. People who activate our throat chakra are religious leaders, teachers, and those who help us use our intellectual abilities.

Because the throat chakra deals with our ability to communicate, 1, The Magician is an apt archetype. At times we must communicate with ourselves so that we can become aware of truths that were apparent all along if we would only observe. Mediation on 9, The Hermit helps us to accomplish this.

Brow Chakra

The brow chakra, or third eye, is located at the centre of the forehead, between the eyebrows. This chakra is associated with the color indigo and is represented by all spirits living or dead. The third eye is the seat of the celestial body, which holds our future and governs clairvoyance or our ability to see beyond space and time. When the brow chakra is open we can see auras or spirit guides, and we can look into the past or future. With the third eye, we gain intuition, imagination, mental abilities, insight, concentration, enlightenment, and heightened perception. When negatively relating to brow chakra issues, we may find ourselves not being able to see life situations clearly or spending our time thinking and analyzing too much.

Physically, the third eye governs the lower brain or cerebellum, central nervous system, vision, eyes, nose, and pituitary gland. When the brow chakra is blocked or maligned we may develop tension headaches, eye problems, or sinus difficulties. Persons who activate our brow chakra are spiritual teachers or friends. Because the brow chakra enables us to see things as they really are we can be inspired with a ray of hope for the future. For this reason 17, The Star is an appropriate archetype. As we develop greater awareness of our surroundings we may decide to utilize the vibrations of 2, The World to finish a scenario that is no longer useful to our growth, and then call upon 0, The Fool to begin afresh. There will, however, be occasions when we are not able to pierce through the veils of our own primary certitudes. It is at these times that we should focus our level of awareness on 18, The Moon so that we can gain greater clarity on what it is we are failing to accurately observe.

Crown Chakra

The crown chakra is located at the top of the head. This chakra is the seat of our etheric body or spiritual realm, and connects us to God, our higher self, or the cosmic consciousness. This chakra is associated with the colors white or violet, and is represented by kachinas or deified ancestral spirits. The crown chakra unifies our higher selves with human personalities, connects us to infinity, and gives us spiritual will, inspiration, unity, divine wisdom and understanding, idealism, and selfless service. When we are not properly relating to crown chakra issues we may find that we lack inspiration, are confused, or hesitate to serve humanity in the manner we have previously agreed to.

Physically, the crown chakra governs our upper brain or cerebrum, pineal gland, cerebral cortex, and central nervous system. If our crown chakra is continuously blocked or not functioning properly we may become depressed and confused. Over an extended period of time this dis-ease in the chakra could result in brain disease or tumors. Persons who tend to activate our crown chakra are spiritual leaders, gurus, saints, and master avatars. Because 10, Wheel of Fortune can be the most fortunate symbol, it is reflective of the higher level of awareness achievable when attuned to this point.

Chakras in the Hands and Feet

Minor energy points are found on the hands and feet. Many healers use these energy channels to heal others mentally, emotionally, and physically by using Reiki, reflexology, aromatherapy, massage, and other alternative therapies. It has been said that meridian points in the hands connect to the heart, so any practitioner should therefore give healing with love and compassion. Because the chakras of our hands and feet deal with our ability to heal others and ourselves, 20, Judgement is the archetypal symbol reflective of these points.

ALL ABOUT SPREADS

The Tarot is a valuable tool that enhances our creativity and problem-solving capabilities. Too often we are not able to see viable alternatives or solutions to problems because we are so enmeshed in the situation we are inquiring about. The simple act of laying a spread forces us to separate ourselves from distractions and concentrate solely on the object of our inquiry. The Tarot allows us to explore alternatives we may not have originally thought of and shows the circumstance in a way that can reveal aspects of the problem previously overlooked. The Tarot can show hidden agendas and solutions we may not have considered, particularly if we are deeply involved in the problem.

Preparing to Use the Tarot

Before using the Tarot you should prepare to give an insightful reading by first centering yourself, using meditation techniques that will help to intensify the mood of the reading and focus your mind. Find a quiet, serene place where you can perform the reading undisturbed. Some people have a special table set aside for such readings, but an accurate reading is possible anywhere.

After centering, hold the Tarot deck in your hands for a few moments to transfer the energy of the question into the deck, and envision yourself enveloped in a protective white light. This white light will protect you from any negative or mischievous energy forms that may try to interfere with the card layout or interpretation. While you are imagining yourself and the Tarot inside the cocoon of white light, say a short prayer to your God, spirit guide, or higher self to help gain insight into the circumstances that prompted the reading, thus helping you to fully interpret the spread.

Feel free to use any system of preparation you feel comfortable with—there are no hard and fast rules for conducting a reading. The main point to remember is that you, the reader, should be centered and removed from the activities of the outside world so that you can give an accurate reading.

If, after attempting to center yourself, you are still unsettled or preoccupied with outside events, you should put the Tarot away and try later when you feel more at ease. Additionally, if you are depressed or feel a lot of negativity around yourself the reading will likely reflect these ambivalent emotions. It is therefore best to try to maintain a positive attitude during the reading, as well as about life in general, to ensure a productive interpretation of the cards.

If you are emotionally involved in the situation that prompted the reading it may be a good idea to ask someone to perform it for you—when we desire a situation to be resolved in a certain way, we may read into the cards what we want them to say instead of what they are really trying to tell us.

When embarking upon any activities that help us to tap into our higher consciousness to gain enlightenment, it is essential that our bodies are as clean as our minds. It is all the more difficult to gain enlightenment when our bodies are polluted with chemicals in the form of alcohol, tobacco, drugs, and even food. Alcohol is a depressant that dulls our senses and loosens our inhibitions. When we smoke cigarettes, our etheric vision is dulled, causing us to perceive situations and events incorrectly. Even food can be harmful when it is abused.

Laying Out the Tarot Spread

After you have prepared yourself for the reading you can begin laying the cards out into the spread that you and the querent have decided upon. Start by shuffling the deck to mingle the energy of the question into the cards. After shuffling, cut the deck into three even piles, using your left hand. The left side of the body is considered the subconscious or intuitive side, so your subconscious will be helping you as you cut the deck. After three equal piles have been formed, select the one that you (or the querent) feel has the answer to the question. Using the left hand, you can begin laying the cards.

An alternate method of laying the cards is to shuffle the deck in the manner described above and spread the entire deck face down across a table or flat surface in a fashion where each individual card can be seen and selected. With the left hand, intuitively pull each card that will be used in the reading.

When a Card Falls Out While Shuffling

When a card falls out while shuffling, it often carries information relevant to the question being asked. The card may either answer the question or provide relevance to the reading. It can add flavor to the question being asked or refer to a different situation entirely.

When a card falls out during the shuffling process you have two options. If you feel that the card is the answer to your question, you can study and interpret it, and then discontinue the reading. If you feel the card simply adds extra insight into the situation you can lay the card to the side and proceed with the reading. When you have finished with the reading you should interpret the card that fell out, as it will give clues to the overall theme of the reading or add extra information that was not included in the spread.

Upright or Reversed Card Laying Methods

Some readers place all of the cards upright while laying a spread while others lay the cards out in the format they were in as they were pulled from the deck. Some Tarot Masters only give card interpretations for the upright position, while others interpret both upright and reversed placements.

In the reversed method each of the seventy-eight cards has two distinct meanings, depending on whether it is laid out in an upright or reversed position, giving you 156 different meanings for the Tarot. The upright method of reading the cards incorporates both the positive and negative meanings and only provides seventy-eight meanings for the entire deck. The Tarot reader must therefore exercise extreme caution not to misinterpret the meaning of a card when performing a reading using this upright method, and should stress both the positive and negative issues surrounding each card.

Some people feel that when reading cards in the reversed position, the routine, day-to-day events of the here and now are being looked at. When reading the cards only in the upright position, however, a more spiritual level of awareness is sought, therefore uncovering elements of a more esoteric nature. When reading the cards, the important thing to remember is that the answer to the question will be revealed by looking at the graphical representation of the archetype portrayed in the card. With this in mind, some people may find attempting to interpret a card distracting when it is upside down.

When to Perform Another Reading

Sometimes it may be necessary to perform an additional reading, which will become evident to the reader during the session. When the card placed in the outcome or result position of the spread is a court card, this indicates that the answer to the question lies with a person associated with that card. After the querent has identified who the person indicated in the reading could be, the reader should perform a second reading, concentrating on how the person in question will influence the situation.

We may perform a Tarot reading where the card in the outcome or result position is ambiguous, and we cannot make out the meaning of the reading. This can be especially so when we are first learning to use the Tarot and have not yet developed the art of visualizing or *picture-thinking*, which is necessary in order to accurately interpret the meanings of the cards. The most direct method of obtaining information for the card is to perform the four-card "What Does This Card Mean?" spread, which gives additional insight into the card's meaning.

Some readers use the same Tarot layout as the original reading to obtain information on the meaning of the card of which they are not sure. For example, if the card in the outcome position of a Celtic Cross reading was vague or inconclusive, the reader would then commence another Celtic Cross reading to gain further insight on the meaning of that particular card. To gain further illumination, many readers place the final card in the previous reading in the first position of the second reading to focus energy into how that particular card will affect the outcome.

There are other times when the reader will find it necessary to perform an additional reading. If a spread of ten cards or less contains more than four cards from the Major Arcana, the reading should be discontinued and a new one begun, using only the cards from the Major Arcana. In drawing more than four cards from the Major Arcana, our higher consciousness is telling us that a higher level of understanding of the Tarot is needed for that particular reading. The Major Arcana alone provides information that is much more spiritual than would normally be gleaned from a spread using the full seventy-eight-card deck. The cards associated with the four suits pertain primarily to normal, day-to-day activities, while the cards from the Major Arcana refer to how our soul is evolving and growing in its present incarnation. A reading using only the twenty-two major arcana indicates that the querent is encountering major life issues, and his or her soul is ready for growth and transformation.

When to Use Only the Major Arcana in a Reading

There may be times when we will want to use only the Major Arcana when giving a reading. These are times when we are going through a period of spiritually significant growth, and a reading using only the Major Arcana will enable us to understand the esoteric influences surrounding us that had prompted us to seek guidance in resolving our problems. These readings will give much insight and clarity into the situation and show the influences that are surreptitiously around us, and which we have overlooked in our attempts to deal with reality.

There will also be times when our higher self is prompting a more meaningful reading that will be readily apparent after the cards have been laid out, such as when four or more major trumps appear. When this occurs, the cards should be picked up and relaid, using only the Major Arcana. A spread of four or more cards from the Major Arcana indicates the reading needs to take place on a more evolved level of understanding. The message derived from such a reading will tend to be much more profound and reveal significant information that is essential to our spiritual growth and evolvement.

Free Will Versus Destiny

Many believe the prediction of an oracle to be permanently engraved in stone, which is simply not the case. Any reading merely gives advice or indicates what is likely to happen if we continue on our current path, but we can change the reading any time we make a conscious decision to do so. The decisions we make daily alter and change our destiny; thus our life paths are fluid and constantly changing with our soul development. If we receive a reading we don't like, we have the ability to use our free will to change its outcome. Conversely, if we receive a reading with a positive outcome, we may need to take certain steps to assure the result that we would like. We have free will over our own destiny and can create any environment or life circumstance that we so choose.

Many querents make the mistake of hanging on to every word a reader says instead of relying on the inherent knowledge each of us possesses. Any reputable reader will advise the client of their free will, and will mention trends he or she is likely to encounter based upon their stage of development during the time of the consultation.

A Word about Ethics

Any person using intuitive abilities in doing a reading must be careful not to predict dire events which could cause the querent serious concern. The Tarot is a very subtle tool and many *negative* events manifesting in the reading may not be quite so devastating when put into proper perspective. An example of this is the Death card in the Major Arcana, which represents transformations and major change. Although the card can in some cases represent an actual death, it often manifests itself as the death of an outmoded concept or idea, allowing for regeneration and rebirth. In such instances, Death may not necessarily predict dire events, but the refinement and attunement of the situation that prompted the reading in the first place. Another card that can be wrongly interpreted is The Tower, which usually means shedding old layers and removing debris to clear the way for positive change. Of course, for positive events to occur some unpleasantness may transpire in the process, but the ultimate result should affirm an improved state of being after the necessary actions have taken place. Additionally, The Lovers, often perceived to represent those soulmate unions we encounter in our lives, could actually indicate a marriage of necessity or a love triangle of some sort. Therefore, we must exercise discretion to properly interpret the cards as they fall, in order to give the querent all possible alternatives.

Readers must be careful not to let their own prejudices interfere, such as when a well-meaning person tries to read for a friend who is going through difficulties and ends up spicing the situation up with his or her own opinions, which is actually a form of manipulation. Many people can be susceptible to suggestion; for this reason the Tarot reader has a great deal of power over the querent when giving a reading. This influence should be used responsibly, and with a great deal of discretion. Most forms of divination, no matter how expertly done, are never totally accurate because we all have free will and are constantly altering the future. Therefore, we should always try to be positive when giving readings, because a negative or pessimistic comment could end up becoming a self-fulfilling prophecy.

It is important to note that a reading should never be performed without a person's permission. When giving an unrequested reading, the reader is invading another's privacy, as well as behaving in a grossly unprofessional manner. It is highly unlikely that an accurate reading could be obtained through such activities, because the energy of the person in question, a vital component for any divination, would be missing and therefore invalidate any interpretations.

Choosing a Significator

The significator is a card in the spread that represents the querent. One of the court cards within the Minor Arcana is normally selected as the significator, but the readings in this work were intentionally modified to make this card unnecessary. The significators were replaced with theme cards because more insight can be gained from the reading if the card is randomly dealt from the deck instead of intentionally selected. The theme card will generally reflect the tone of the situation, and further illuminates the reading as a whole.

If the reader would rather use a significator, he only needs to replace the theme card, which is selected at random, with the significator, which is pulled from the deck before shuffling and dealing.

While the significator is normally one of the court cards, some readers prefer using cards from the Major Arcana because they are considered to represent more highly evolved archetypal entities and therefore bring us to a more spiritual level of being.

Significators in the Minor Arcana

Page of Wands	A young woman or child who is Aries, Leo, or Sagittarius
Knight of Wands	A young man who is Aries, Leo, or Sagittarius
Queen of Wands	A mature woman who is Aries, Leo, or Sagittarius
King of Wands	A mature man who is Aries, Leo, or Sagittarius

Page of Pentacles	A young woman or child who is Taurus, Virgo, or Capricorn
Knight of Pentacles	A young man who is Taurus, Virgo or Capricorn
Queen of Pentacles	A mature woman who is Taurus, Virgo or Capricorn
King of Pentacles	A mature man who is Taurus, Virgo, or Capricorn
Page of Swords	A young woman or child who is Gemini, Libra, or Aquarius
Knight of Swords	A young man who is Gemini, Libra, or Aquarius
Queen of Swords	A mature woman who is Gemini, Libra, or Aquarius
King of Swords	A mature man who is Gemini, Libra, or Aquarius
Page of Cups	A young woman or child who is Cancer, Scorpio, or Pisces
Knight of Cups	A young man who is Cancer, Scorpio, or Pisces
Queen of Cups	A mature woman who is Cancer, Scorpio, or Pisces
King of Cups	A mature man who is Cancer, Scorpio, or Pisces

Significators in the Major Arcana

The Magician	A young man
The High Priestess	A young woman
The Empress	An older or mature woman
The Emperor	An older or mature man

Tarot Journal

To fully understand how the Tarot applies to our lives, it is useful to keep a Tarot Journal, recording the date, question asked, the spread, interpretation of the cards, and any notes for future reference. When we ask the Tarot a specific question and record it in our journal, we can later review the answer to see how the readings have unfolded and ultimately revealed the truth that we needed to know.

A Tarot journal helps us to remember the meanings of the cards, as the very act of recording the reading is an invaluable tool for memory improvement, and will help us learn the more intricate meanings of the cards. When we can remember the meanings of the cards without the aid of reference material then we are on our way to giving competent readings for others.

Spreads to Try

When Tarot students are just beginning their journey, they may not understand the full meaning of a card that has been drawn. The "What Does This Card Mean?" spread shown first in this section is a very simple four-card spread that is useful for gaining insight into the card's relevance. The spreads that follow it are tailored to specific circumstances or questions, and, used in conjunction with the chapters related to specific areas of symbolism will assist readers to perform successful readings.

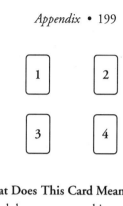

What Does This Card Mean? Spread

Card 1: The card does not mean this.

Card 2: The card means this.

Card 3: The card is good for this.

Card 4: The best course of action.

The Elemental Tarot Spread

The Elemental Tarot spread is a short reading that can be used stand-alone or to begin a more extended session. The spread consists of five cards that are detailed below:

Card 1, Fire: Fire indicates what business areas we are likely to be concerned with. This position can also depict psychic or creative endeavors we are actively involved in. This position can depict our romantic associations, relationships with children, or upcoming holiday plans.

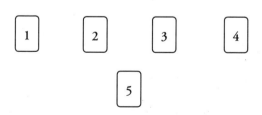

The Elemental Tarot Spread

Card 2, Earth: Earth indicates our financial or material situation. This position denotes our possessions, values, or self-esteem. The earth position shows how we handle our duties, responsibilities, or career path.

Card 3, Air: Air indicates how we communicate with others. This communication can be light and social, intimate, or informational. The position of air gives an indication of how we relate to partners, friends, or acquaintances. This position may depict what we can expect from correspondence or legal proceedings.

Card 4, Water: Water indicates our emotional state of being and shows what areas are most likely to evoke an emotional response. Water depicts our home life and those areas which need refinement.

Card 5, Spirit: Spirit represents issues that tend to be karmic in nature. Spirit shows areas which go beyond our day-to-day activities but seem destined in some way. This position indicates areas we have chosen to encounter in order to help us progress along our spiritual path.

The Astro House Tarot Spread

The Astro House Tarot Spread can be used to find out what issues center around the twelve major spheres in our life. Thirteen cards are laid out, the first twelve cards indicate the areas of life to be covered and the thirteenth represents the overall theme of the reading.

Card 1: The first house represents our personality, self, and behavior.

Card 2: The second house represents our possessions, values, and sensuality.

Card 3: The third house represents our ability to communicate, short travels, and learning.

Card 4: The fourth house represents our home, security, and a parental guidance.

Card 5: The fifth house represents our love life, creativity, and relationship with children.

Card 6: The sixth house represents our duties, responsibilities, and state of health.

Card 7: The seventh house represents our marriage, close friends, open enemies, contracts, and other legal agreements.

Card 8: The eighth house represents the our sexuality, major changes, joint resources, and death.

Card 9: The ninth house represents our religious preferences and philosophy, college education, travels, and experiences that form our outlook on life.

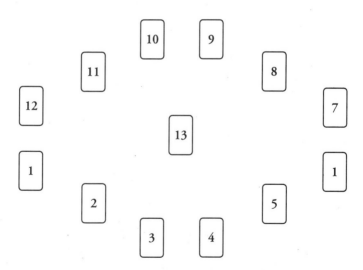

The Astro House Tarot Spread

Card 10: The tenth house represents our career, reputation, success, and destiny in life.

Card 11: The eleventh house represents our life goals, friendships, and associations.

Card 12: The twelfth house represents our karma, secret enemies, troubles, and our own self-undoing.

Card 13: The overall theme of the reading.

Astro Month Tarot Spread

The Astro Month Tarot Spread is another reading that can be used to depict trends developing during the course of the year. This spread utilizes thirteen cards, with twelve cards representing the months in the year and the thirteenth card illustrates the overall trend of the reading. The layout is identical to the Astro House Spread on page 201.

Card 1: January; Card 2: February; Card 3: March; Card 4: April; Card 5: May; Card 6: June; Card 7: July; Card 8: August; Card 9: September; Card 10: October; Card 11: November; Card 12: December; Card 13: Theme of the reading.

The Triple Astro House Spread

After becoming confident with the fundamentals of the Astro House Spread, it would be advantageous to experiment with the Triple Astro House Spread because it contains thirty-nine cards that will reveal greater clarification on issues that are fuzzy. The layout for this spread is identical to that of the Astro House Spread, but each position contains three cards instead of one. They are grouped as follows:

Cards 1, 14, 27; Cards 2, 15, 28; Cards 3, 16, 29; Cards 4, 17, 30; Cards 5, 18, 31; Cards 6, 19, 32; Cards 7, 20, 33; Cards 8, 21, 34; Cards 9, 22, 35; Cards 10, 23, 36; Cards 11, 24, 37; Cards 12, 25, 38; Cards 13, 26, 39.

The Triple Astro Month Spread

The layout for this spread is identical to the Triple Astro Month Spread as described above.

Six Months Spread at a Glance

The Six Months Spread (see page 204) is suitable for those who would like to know about the coming half year ahead.

Column A, the Self: The three cards in this column state the circumstances of our life at the time of the reading. It tells of our emotional state, what is occupying our mind and what our primary concerns are.

Column B, Relationships: The three cards in this column give an indication of the status of our personal relationships at the time of the reading. These relationships generally refer to our partners, close friends, and even enemies. If the cards laid out in this column are impersonal, then close relationships may not be important at the time of the reading. If this is the case, then this column refers to our general environment.

Column C, Hopes/fears and dreams/wishes: The three cards in this column indicate our hopes, fears, dreams and wishes.

Column D, Expectations: The three cards in this position indicate what we expect to occur in the next six months. Because these cards reflect only our expectations, the events portrayed may be delayed, or never even transpire.

Column E, Unexpected Events: The three cards which appear in this column show us the events which are unexpected. These cards often reveal destiny or karmic related issues.

Column F, Near Future: The three cards in this column indicate events which are likely to transpire within the next two or three months from the time of the reading.

Column G, Distant Future: The three cards which appear in this column reveal the events which are likely to transpire within the next four to six months from the time of the reading. The cards in columns four, five, and six provide clues as to how the events are related.

Card 22, Theme: The final card drawn depicts the overall theme of the coming six month period. If selected randomly, it can provide valuable insight into how the querent can best deal and relate to this time.

Row 1

Row 2

Row 3

A   B   C   D   E   F   G

22

The Six Months Spread

The Romany Spread

The Romany Spread is another reading that gives insight into events which are likely to transpire during the coming half year. The Romany Spread is identical to the Six Months Spread shown on page 204, and utilizes twenty-two cards which are divided into three horizontal rows, covering the past, present, and future, with the last card (22) representing the theme of the reading.

Row 1, the Past: The cards that fall in this row indicate prominent events which have led up to the reading and how they impact our life.

Row 2, the Present: The cards that fall in this row depict events which seem to affect us at the time of the reading.

Row 3, the Future: The cards that fall in this position illustrate events which are likely to transpire within the next six month period following the reading.

Daily Tarot Spreads

The Tarot can be used as a very powerful meditative tool as well as a divinatory device, and a reading can simply consist of one card. This card, pulled at the beginning or end of each day can reveal valuable insights into the archetypal themes we encounter in our daily life. Two spreads that can be used on a daily basis are the One-Card Daily Reading and the Three-Card Daily Reading.

The One-Card Daily Reading

The One-Card Daily Reading is a simple spread that can easily be performed at the beginning or end of each day. The querent only needs to ask what he needs to know for the day while shuffling and pulling a card from the deck. It is useful to record the date of the reading and card into your Tarot Journal because often the full meaning will not become apparent for some time. With the reading recorded in the journal, it can later be referred to for verification as well as a better understanding of surrounding events.

The Three-Card Daily Reading

The Three-Card Daily reading can be used to help assess the workings of three areas of our lives which are the physical, mental, and spiritual realms. Although the Three-Card Daily Reading takes a little longer to perform than the One-Card Daily Reading, it does give greater clarity. The Three-Card Spread is performed as follows.

Card 1. Where am I physically?

Card 2. Where am I mentally?

Card 3. Where am I spiritually.

Physical   Mental   Spiritual

The Three-Card Daily Spread

The Seven-Pointed Star

The Seven-Pointed Star is a popular spread (shown on page 207) used to determine significant events which are likely to transpire during a week. The Seven-Pointed Star is an eight-card spread that can be performed to highlight the important events for the coming week. The first seven cards reflect the issues for each day of the week, while the eighth provides the essence of the week as a whole.

Card 1: Monday; Card 2: Tuesday; Card 3: Wednesday; Card 4: Thursday; Card 5: Friday; Card 6: Saturday; Card 7: Sunday; Card 8: Theme.

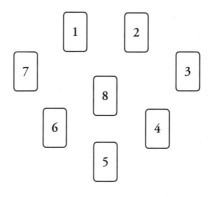

The Seven-Pointed Star Spread

The Celtic Cross Spread

The Celtic Cross is an ancient oracle that is one of the most widely used spreads today (see page 208). It can be used to answer specific questions or provide a general reading. The basic Celtic Cross is composed of ten cards.

Card 1, the Question: This card denotes the nature of the question and can often reflect entirely different motives than what we were originally concerned about.

Card 2, the Influence: This card position denotes the atmosphere, which has a direct bearing on the reading. It also reflects those circumstances which are at cross-purposes to the attainment of our goals and ambitions.

Card 3, the Background: This card position depicts the situation that prompted us to request a reading.

Card 4, the Recent Past: This card position indicates events that have occurred prior to the reading and have a direct bearing on the situation.

Card 5, the Present: This card position represents the present feelings, hopes, and fears at the time of the reading.

Card 6, the Near Future: This card position shows us what is likely to happen in the very near future, usually up to three months.

Card 7, the Querent's Attitude: This card position denotes our attitude regarding the situation.

Card 8, Other's Views: This card position denotes how other people close to us perceive the situation and depicts the environment in which we find ourselves surrounded.

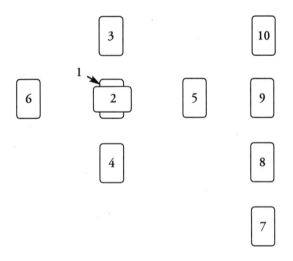

The Celtic Cross Spread

Card 9, Pros and Cons: This card position presents a detached view the benefits and pitfalls of the situation.

Card 10, the Outcome: This card position depicts the probable outcome. It should be stressed at this point that if the card which falls in the outcome position is not desirable, we have the power of our own free will to change our circumstances in any way we see fit because this card only gives an indication of what is expected to come about should all elements remain unchanged.

The Triple Celtic Cross Spread

The Celtic Cross is an excellent spread which has withstood the test of time. Many readers have been using variations of this oracle since antiquity. The more advanced student of Tarot may like to glean more information from the Celtic Cross and will find the Triple Celtic Cross to be quite informative. It is identical to the traditional Celtic Cross except that three cards are placed in each position instead of one. They are grouped as follows:

Cards 1, 11, 21; Cards 2, 12, 22; Cards 3, 13, 23; Cards 4, 14, 24; Cards 5, 15, 25; Cards 6, 16, 26; Cards 7, 17, 27; Cards 8, 18, 28; Cards 9, 19, 29; Cards 10, 20, 30.

The Celtic Block Spread

The Celtic Block is a continuation of the Celtic Cross where an additional four cards are drawn to add greater clarity and meaning to the reading (see page 210). Cards 11, 12, and 13 make up the Triad and represent subtle influences surrounding the querent. Card 14 is the Solidifier, and formulates the previous thirteen cards and the outcome of the reading. The Solidifier should serve the purpose of clarifying or verifying all previous indications uncovered.

The Celtic Block is a separate reading from the Celtic Cross, so a conscious decision to perform the Celtic Block must therefore be made before laying the spread. If the Celtic Cross is laid out and the additional four cards are drawn as an afterthought, the triad and solidifier may give contradictory results because the subtle energies inherent in the original question were not shuffled into the deck during the preparation process.

Cards 11, 12, 13, Triad: These cards depict subtle influences surrounding the querent's emotions, attitudes, and associations.

Card 14, Solidifier: This card serves to solidify the interpretation gleaned from the previous thirteen cards. It should compliment and add to the information obtained from card 10, the outcome.

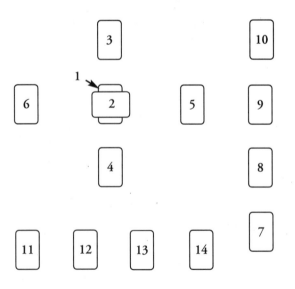

The Celtic Block Spread

The Ankh Spread

People generally seek the Tarot's guidance when they are searching the truth to a particular matter, and in ancient Egyptian mythology the ankh was considered to be a symbol of eternal life yoked by incarnation into the human form. This ancient symbol also represents wisdom and truth. The Ankh Spread is very popular in Germany, where cognitive psychology and gestalt therapy was initially developed. This spread is an invaluable tool when seeking conscious and unconscious levels of knowledge about a given circumstance.

The Ankh Spread is composed of nine cards that explore the higher psychological issues revolving around the situation that prompted the reading.

Card 1, Attitude: This position represents an attitude, impulse, or energy which is inherent within the situation. It can represent unconscious thoughts, so its meaning may not be readily apparent.

Card 2, a second Attitude: This card position represents a second attitude, impulse, or energy, which is inherent within the situation. Like card 1, it can also represent unconscious thoughts, so its meaning may not be readily apparent. Sometimes it compliments card 1 and at others it will pose a contradictory viewpoint if the situation concerns a group of people with differing ideas.

Card 3, Early Causes: This card position reflects the initial influences, which led to the reading. These early causes could date back anywhere from one to several years, or even past lives if the reading is of a karmic nature.

Card 4, Trigger: The card drawn and placed in this position is the catalyst that brought the situation to our awareness.

Card 5, Higher Cognition: The card in this position indicates our higher cognition and shows what we know to be the truth in our higher awareness.

Card 6, Inevitable Consequence: This card position shows us what events had to inevitably transpire based upon the attitudes prevalent in the previous five cards. In most cases, the event this card portrays is readily apparent to us because it had a direct impact on our sphere of awareness.

Card 7, the Next Step: This card position indicates what needs to transpire next within the sequence of events

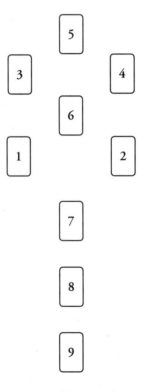

The Ankh Spread

making up the situation. Sometimes this placement reflects a specific action we must take or a meeting that must take to resolve the dilemma.

Card 8, a Surprising Experience: This card position reflects an unexpected surprise which will ultimately influence the outcome.

Card 9, Probable Outcome: This card position indicates the probable outcome of the situation in question.

The Tree of Life Spread

The Tree of Life Spread is based upon the Cabalistic trestle-board called The Tree of Life. This spread contains 10 cards that correlate to the ten sephiram in the Tree of Life. This spread is useful when beginning a session because it gives a clear indication of the our general focus at the time of the reading.

Card 1: Corresponds to Kether, which represents our spiritual world and inner state of being.

Card 2: Corresponds to Chokmah, which relates to our energy, drive, or areas of responsibility.

Card 3: Corresponds with Binah, which represents the areas in life where we face limitations, restrictions, or issues, which he must learn to stabilize.

Card 4: Corresponds with Chesed, which represents financial matters and practical activities.

Card 5: Corresponds with Geburah, which denotes strife, challenges, and the areas we feel opposition to.

Card 6: Corresponds with Tipareth, which represents the areas in life where we are successful and receives acclaim.

Card 7: Corresponds with Netzach, which represents our love life, attractions, and emotional attachments.

Card 8: Corresponds with Hod, which indicates worldly matters, business, and career pursuits. It also indicates how we approach those endeavors.

Card 9: Corresponds with Yesod, which refers to our unconscious mind and areas in life which are hidden.

Card 10: Corresponds with Malkuth, which refers to our roots, family life, and close relationships.

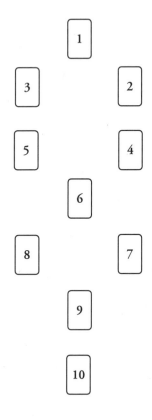

The Tree of Life Spread

The Pathway Spread

The Pathway Spread is based upon the twenty-two pathways that connect the ten sephiram in the Cabala (see page 150), and should not be performed very often because it places much esoteric significance into our lives and will tend to stay with us for quite some time. The Pathway Spread can be used in conjunction with the Tree of Life Spread to give a meaningful reading descriptive of the esoteric influences which surround us. It is a twenty-two-card layout that can be performed using the complete deck or the Major Arcana alone.

When using only the twenty-two cards of the Major Arcana to perform a reading of such significance, it should be considered a life reading, in that the circumstances that surround the entire theme of our life will prevail. The entire seventy-eight card deck can be used to perform an annual reading that will reflect the themes we will encounter in the year for which the reading has been performed.

> Card 1: This position presents those choices we will be asked to make along our life path. Although we come into the earth plane with a set agenda of what areas we are supposed to explore, we are also given free choice to change our destination along our spiritual journey.
>
> Card 2: This position represents those tools we have been given to help us accomplish the tasks we have agreed to before being born into the earth plane.
>
> Card 3: This position represents the inner knowledge we have within us to solve problems we encounter in our daily Earth walk.
>
> Card 4: This position symbolizes the feminine within us as well as the matriarchal role models we will encounter in our Earth walk.

Card 5: This position symbolizes the masculine within us as well as the patriarchal role models we will encounter in our earth walk.

Card 6: This position represents our philosophical outlook on life and those persons who will serve as mentors to us.

Card 7: This card indicates what areas we are likely to find the greatest enjoyment in, and those persons we are reunited with in this life who are our soulmates from previous incarnations.

Card 8: This position represents those areas in life where we need to steadily persist, even in the most trying of circumstances because success will eventually come through effort and dedication.

Card 9: This position represents those areas in life where we need to exercise discipline and strength to more fully develop our sense of self.

Card 10: This position indicates what areas we need to search within ourselves to find solutions to dilemmas we encounter.

Card 11: This position indicates areas that seem destined or fated. It seems that events transpire to bring about inevitabilities which we have agreed to encounter long before incarnating into this plane of existence.

Card 12: This position indicates the areas we need to seek balance and harmony. It serves to warn us of any issues, which may require balance.

Card 13: This position indicates the area where we will be asked to make a sacrifice, bringing much wisdom and a greater level of understanding, which we would not have obtained otherwise.

Card 14: This position indicates those areas where we must experience a radical transformation which will ultimately bring about much-needed growth after the dust has settled.

Card 15: This position indicates those areas where we need to practice moderation.

Card 16: This position represents those areas where we seem to be bound to and experience a deep sense of obligation that we would rather be free from. It is also indicative of those situations where we will be tempted to take a certain course of action even when we know that to do so would be detrimental to our spiritual growth.

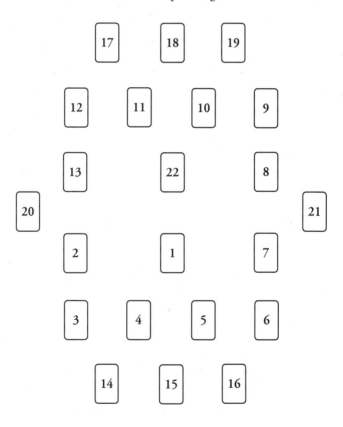

The Pathway Spread

Card 17: This position indicates those areas in which we need to be uprooted and make a clean break because we have become complacent. While these upheavals are often unsettling, they will bring about much needed growth, which we would not otherwise have pursued without provocation.

Card 18: This position indicates those areas where we are quite knowledgeable and can pass our expertise on to others. It is also the wish card, which enables some of our dreams to come true.

Card 19: This position reveals those areas in our lives where we have been unrealistic and cannot see the situation we are involved in clearly. It relates to those elements that will cause us to become depressed as well as those persons we encounter who are deceptive in their intentions towards us.

Card 20: This position indicates those areas that will bring much happiness and joy.

Card 21: This position reveals karma brought over from past lives that we have agreed to work on in this life to enable us to clear any debts and replenish our souls.

Card 22: This position reveals the task we have incarnated into the earth plane to complete. According to the laws of reincarnation, we are not randomly put into an environment, but instead have a free hand in selecting the circumstances that will give us the most growth to allow us to complete our earth purpose.

The Chakra Spread

The Chakra Spread allows us to assess the conditions of our chakras. Chakras alternately open and close, depending on our state of being. Negative thoughts or emotions also have a tendency to block chakras, so these blockages therefore need to be identified and resolved. When these issues are addressed and remedied, the chakras should begin to function normally again. The Chakra Spread utilizes ten cards, each representing one of the major chakras in the body.

Card 1, Root Chakra: This card position indicates what areas in life are affecting our sense of security. It shows how our survival instincts surface when we are under pressure or feel threatened. This card position indicates how we relate to your physical world and what materialistic areas we are presently working on. The root chakra position also indicates how we relate to family members.

Card 2, Sacral Plexus: This card position indicates issues that are affecting our emotional well-being. It indicates what our sex life is like and what lessons we need to learn concerning our sexuality. The sacral plexus position also indicates the relationship we have with those who bring out strong emotional or sexual feelings.

Card 3, Solar Plexus: This card position revolves around issues affecting our ability to stay centered. It shows what circumstances we need to be aware of which have the potential to affect our life. The solar plexus position indicates the relationship we have with those who have an impact on our lifestyle and livelihood.

Card 4, Heart Chakra: This card position shows our ability to give and receive love. It indicates our capacity to trust and what areas we need to show empathy. The heart chakra placement shows what lessons we must encounter in learning to love unconditionally and our relationship with those who come into our lives to act as mirrors.

Card 5, Thymus Chakra: This card position indicates what areas of life are affecting our ability to be at peace with ourselves. It shows what circumstances are causing stress and are thus affecting our body's immune system. The thymus position tells what lessons we are facing to better enable us to learn compassion for others and the relationship we have with those people.

The Chakra Spread

Card 6, Throat Chakra: This card position indicates our ability to communicate. It shows what areas we need to listen very carefully, as well as convey our true message when speaking or writing. The throat chakra spread shows our relationship with those who stimulate our ability to communicate.

Card 7, Brow Chakra: This card position indicates what areas of life we need to take a closer look at. Are we seeing things clearly and as they really are? The brow chakra position also shows what areas we can use our imagination to expand our creativity.

Card 8, Crown Chakra: This card position indicates how our spirituality is developing and shows what obstacles are keeping us from fully connecting to our higher self.

Card 9, Hand Chakra: This card position gives us an indication of how we can use our energy to heal others and make the world a better place to live in. It may indicate who or what type of person we can send our loving thoughts to which will help them more fully follow their path.

Card 10, Foot Chakra: This card position shows us what areas we need to stay grounded because there are some turbulent times ahead, and we need to steady ourselves so that we do not become disillusioned or deceived.

The Horseshoe Spread

The Horseshoe Spread (page 223) is useful when asking questions of a specific or general nature. It contains only seven cards and is therefore suitable for beginners. There are three basic versions of the Horseshoe Spread; the Classic Horseshoe, which is used to answer general questions; the Work Horseshoe, which is used to answer work and career related questions; and the Love Horseshoe, which is used to answer questions related to love and romance. All of the Horseshoe spreads use the same layout pattern.

Card 1, the Past: This position indicates past events that have a direct bearing on the question.

Card 2, the Present: This position depicts feelings, thoughts, or events that directly relate to the present situation.

Card 3, Hidden Influences: This position indicates hidden influences that could surprise the querent or alter the outcome of the situation.

Card 4, Obstacles: This position shows the querent which obstacles, of a mental or physical nature, he or she needs to overcome in order to have a successful outcome.

Card 5, the Environment: This position depicts surrounding influences, the attitudes of others, and the general environment that the querent is currently facing.

Card 6, Best Course of Action: This position directs the querent to the best course of action in order to have a satisfactory result.

Card 7, Probable Outcome: This position indicates the probable outcome of the situation, providing the querent follows the advice given in Card 6, which counsels him or her on the best course of action.

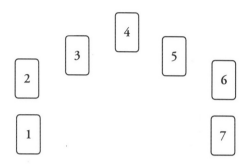

The Horseshoe Spread

The Work Horseshoe Spread

Card 1, the Past: This position indicates past influences affecting the querent's problem, dilemma, or question.

Card 2, the Present: This position indicates the present situation the querent is encountering relating to his work or career.

Card 3, Positively: This position indicates what is most positive regarding the situation. This can include talents, abilities, security, or wealth.

Card 4, Negativity: This position indicates what is difficult about the situation. These difficulties could range from lack of experience, low self-confidence, boredom, lack of sufficient material gain, or difficulties with bosses or coworkers. If a positive card appears in this position then there are likely to be few difficulties related to the matter.

Card 5, Outside Factors: This position reflects outside influences relating to the situation.

Card 6, Best Course: This position indicates the best course of action the querent can take.

Card 7, Outcome: This position indicates the probable outcome to the situation, providing the querent follows the counsel given in card 6.

The Love Horseshoe Spread

The Love Horseshoe is an excellent spread to perform when we have questions of a romantic nature.

Card 1, the Past: This position indicates the foundation of the relationship.

Card 2, the Present: This position shows how the querent sees the relationship.

Card 3, Hopes, Fears, and Expectations: This position shows what beliefs the querent is bringing into the relationship. It may also show the unconscious elements, attitudes or patterns of behavior.

Card 4, Conflicts: This position indicates areas of conflict that can be emotional, mental or financial. This placement can also alert the querent to possible conflicts between family, career, or friends.

Card 5, Outside Influences: This position indicates outside influences which could affect the relationship. These influences include previous marriages or relationships, parents or children, friends or social activities, or even infidelities that the querent may not be aware of.

Card 6, Best Course: This position denotes the best course of action the querent should take regarding the relationship.

Card 7, Probable Outcome: This position indicates the probable outcome of the situation, providing the querent follows the counsel given by Card 6.

The Quick Spread

There will inevitably be occasions when there is not enough time available to perform one of the more complex readings such as the Celtic Cross or Astro House Spread; during these times that a quick reading is preferable. The following spread contains only three cards and is useful in determining the outcome of projects, events, or relationships in a short time.

Card 1, the Past: Past circumstances that have a direct bearing on the question.

Card 2, the Present: The present situation and what can be done to bring about a favorable outcome.

Card 3, Outcome: The probable outcome of the situation.

The Quick Spread

"Yes or No" and the Tarot

There are many spreads, such as the Celtic Cross and Horseshoe Spread, which give a detailed answer to the question asked, to include delving into the causes, hidden influences, and pros and cons of the situation that prompted the reading. These spreads are useful in helping to get to the root of the problem, but can be quite time consuming as well.

Sometimes when in a rush we merely want a simple yes or no, and are not too terribly concerned about surrounding influences. It is during these times that the quick Yes/No Spread can be very useful. Some questions that can be asked using this spread are:

Should I move to . . . ?

Should I take such and such a course at college?

Will I receive payment this week?

Will I receive notification about my new job this week?

How to perform the reading: shuffle the question into the deck of cards. Spread the entire seventy-eight cards out on the table, face down. Intuitively select three cards from the deck and put the remaining cards to the side and out of the way. Turn the three cards over. The answer to the question depends on how many of the cards are right-side-up.

Three cards right-side-up: If three cards are right-side-up, then the answer to the question is yes.

One or two cards right-side-up: If two cards are right-side-up, then the answer to the question is not certain. Circumstances surrounding the question have not yet transpired to bring about a definitive answer. The future is fluid and constantly changing, and the outcome depends upon decisions, which have not been made at the time of the reading.

No cards right-side-up: If no cards are right-side-up, the answer to the question is no.

This three-card spread is fast and easy, and gives a quick response to a query that needs a simple yes or no answer. Although it is not necessary to interpret the cards, which have been intuitively drawn, they usually have direct relevance to the question being asked and can shed more light on the situation.

The Soulmate Search Spread

The Tarot can help show people the paths they and their partners will take before meeting and uniting with each other. The Tarot can be used to accurately predict the soulmates we will encounter while in this incarnation with the Soulmate Search being a powerful spread that can be used to help us (see page 228). The Soulmate Search is an in-depth spread that depicts our soul urges and should not be used frequently because we rarely encounter such persons in our life paths. This spread should be performed no more than once a year and recorded for future reference.

Before proceeding with the Soulmate Search, it is essential to clarify some facts about soulmates. During our life we normally encounter several soulmates or partners who teach us lessons and help us develop. If we do not meet and accept the challenges provided by our soulmate, or we grow in different directions, then the relationship will stagnate. If we are not able to change as the relationship evolves, it may become unrevivable and a crucial decision will need to be made as to whether to stay in the relationship or move on to another. Because this is an era of rapid growth, we tend to enter into as well as dissolve many more relationships than would have been the norm in previous generations.

Cards 1 and 2, Anima or Female Archetype: These positions indicate the feminine side of ourselves. It refers to our emotional responsiveness, our maternal upbringing, and female role models we will meet along our life path.

Cards 3 and 4, Animus or Male Archetype: These positions indicate the masculine side of ourselves. It refers to our intellectual processes, our paternal upbringing, and male role models we will meet along our path.

Cards 5 through 11: The cards that are in this position symbolize the physical, mental, and emotional path our soulmate must encounter before he or she is ready to meet us. The sequence of events as portrayed by the cards normally occurs in chronological order.

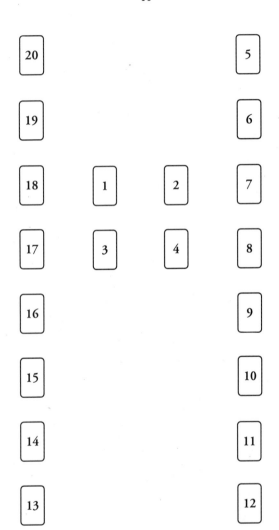

The Soulmate Search Spread

Card 12: This position indicates the nature of the relationship with our soulmate and the ultimate conclusion of the union.

Cards 13 through 20: The cards that fall in this position show the areas of emotional, physical, and mental development that we must experience before we are secure in the relationship.

The Relationship Spread

When a person is already deeply involved in a close relationship he may have questions concerning the outcome of that partnership in particular. The Relationship Spread is a useful tool which gives guidance about the inner workings of the union. The relationship spread is a twenty-two-card reading which speaks of the nature of the bond and its past, present, and future.

Card 1: This position reflects the basis of the union.

Card 2: This position reflects the past circumstances surrounding the union.

Card 3: This position reflects the present circumstances of the union.

Card 4: This position reflects the probable future of the union.

Cards 5 to 7: These positions reflect the past circumstances of partner A.

Cards 8 to 10: These positions reflect the present circumstances of partner B.

Cards 11 to 13: These positions reflect the future circumstances surrounding partner A.

Cards 14 to 16: These positions reflect the past circumstances of partner B.

Cards 17 to 19: These positions reflect the present circumstances of partner B.

Cards 20 to 22: These positions reflect the future circumstances surrounding partner B.

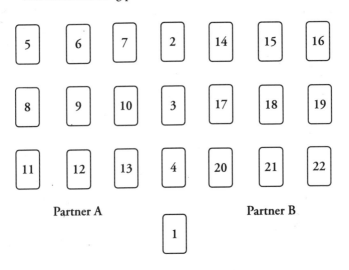

The Relationship Spread

The Runic Tarot Spread

Quite often people pull a single rune, called Odin's Rune, to gain insight into specific life situations. Odin's Rune will, as a rule, provide sufficient information to enable us to proceed with the right action and skillful means. There will be times, however, when the need to know extends beyond the authority of a single stone. This five-rune spread breaks down the distinctive features of a situation that might overwhelm us with its complexity or uncertainty, giving us a highly personal and specific reading.

The Runic Tarot Spread is based on the five-rune spread. The runes in the spread are replaced with Tarot cards, adding a bit of flavor to this Scandinavian oracle. The spread follows:

Card 1: Overview of the situation.

Card 2: The querent's challenge.

Card 3: Best course of action.

Card 4: A sacrifice that needs to be made.

Card 5: A new situation evolving.

| 1 | 2 | 3 | 4 | 5 |

The Runic Tarot Spread

The Pyramid Spread

The final spread in this book has somewhat of an Egyptian flair, as it has been designed in the shape of a pyramid. It is useful when you have a specific question or problem that needs a resolution to, and is laid out as follows:

Card 1: Aspect or influence that prompted reading.

Cards 2–3: Options or alternatives available to the querent.

Cards 4–6: Forces at work that give rise to the situation.

Cards 7–10: The best way to handle the situation.

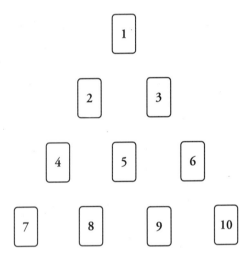

The Pyramid Spread

Recommended Reading

Adam and the Kabbalistic Tree, by Z'ev ben Shimon Halevi. Gateway Books, Bath.

The Anatomy of Fate, by Z'ev ben Shimon Halevi. Arkana, London.

The Angels Within Us, by John Randolph Price. Fawcett Columbine, New York.

The Anointed, by Z'ev ben Shimon Halevi. Gateway Books, Bath.

An Introduction to Practical Astronomy, by Brian Jones. The Apple Press, London.

Ask Your Angels, by Alma Daniel et al. Ballantine, USA.

Astrology from A to Z, by Eleanor Bach. Allied Books, New York.

The Chakra Handbook, by Shalila Sharamon and Bodoj Baginski. Lotus Light Publications, USA.

Chart Your Own Horoscope, by Ursula Lewis. Grosset and Dunlap, New York.

Discover Numerology, by Julia Line. Harper Collins Publishers, London.

Discover Tarot, by Emily Peach. Harper Collins Publishers, London.

Elemental Tarot, by Caroline Smith and John Astrop. Bantam Doubleday Dell Publishing Group, New York.

Godwin's Cabalistic Encyclopedia, by David Godwin. Llewellyn Publications, St Paul, Minnesota.

Honey From the Rock, by Lawrence Kushmer. Jewish Lights Publishing, Woodstock, Vermont.

The Illustrated I Ching, by R. L. Wing. Doubleday, New York.

I Ching, by John Blofeld. Harper Collins Publishers, New York.

The Kwan Yin Book of Changes, by Diane Stein. Llewellyn Publications, St. Paul, Minnesota.

Linda Goodman's Star Signs, by Linda Goodman. St. Martin's Press, New York.

Live your Life by the Numbers, by Sylvia di Pietro. Signet, USA.

The Living Stars, by Dr. Eric Morse. Amethyst Books, New York.

Mastering the Tarot, by Eden Grey. Signet Books, New York.

Numerology, by Harish Johari. Destiny Books, Rochester, Vermont.

The Pictorial Key to the Tarot, by A. E. Waite. Parragon Book Service, London.

Tarot, by Jane Lyle. Mallard Press, USA.

The Tarot, by Nancy Shavick. Berkley Books, New York.

Tarot, a New Handbook for the Apprentice, by Eileen Connolly. Aquarian Press, England.

The Tarot Guide to Love and Relationships, by Nancy Shavick. Berkley Books, New York.

The Tarot Reader, by Nancy Shavick. Berkley Books, New York.

Tarot, the Handbook for the Journeyman, by Eileen Connolly. Aquarian Press, England.

Traveling the Royal Road, by Nancy Shavick. Berkley Books, New York.

The Truth About Cabala, by David Godwin. Llewellyn Publications, St. Paul, Minnesota.

The Wheel of Destiny, by Patricia McLaine. Llewellyn Publications, St. Paul, Minnesota.

Index

☽ REACH FOR THE MOON

Llewellyn publishes hundreds of books on your favorite subjects! To get these exciting books, including the ones on the following pages, check your local bookstore or order them directly from Llewellyn.

ORDER BY PHONE
- Call toll-free within the U.S. and Canada, 1-800-THE MOON
- In Minnesota, call (651) 291-1970
- We accept VISA, MasterCard, and American Express

ORDER BY MAIL
- Send the full price of your order (MN residents add 7% sales tax) in U.S. funds, plus postage & handling to:

  Llewellyn Worldwide
  P.O. Box 64383, Dept. K574-6
  St. Paul, MN 55164–0383, U.S.A.

POSTAGE & HANDLING
(For the U.S., Canada, and Mexico)
- $4.00 for orders $15.00 and under
- $5.00 for orders over $15.00
- No charge for orders over $100.00

We ship UPS in the continental United States. We ship standard mail to P.O. boxes. Orders shipped to Alaska, Hawaii, The Virgin Islands, and Puerto Rico are sent first-class mail. Orders shipped to Canada and Mexico are sent surface mail.

International orders: Airmail—add freight equal to price of each book to the total price of order, plus $5.00 for each non-book item (audio tapes, etc.).

Surface mail—Add $1.00 per item.

Allow 2 weeks for delivery on all orders.
Postage and handling rates subject to change.

DISCOUNTS
We offer a 20% discount to group leaders or agents. You must order a minimum of five copies of the same book to get our special quantity price.

FREE CATALOG
Get a free copy of our color catalog, *New Worlds of Mind and Spirit*. Subscribe for just $10.00 in the United States and Canada ($30.00 overseas, airmail). Many bookstores carry *New Worlds*—ask for it!

Visit our website at www.llewellyn.com for more information.

Tarot: Your Everyday Guide
Practical Problem Solving and Everyday Advice

Janina Renee

Whenever people begin to read the Tarot, they inevitably find themselves asking the cards, "What should I do about such-and-such situation?" Yet there is little information available on how to get those answers from the cards.

Reading the tarot for advice requires a different approach than reading for prediction, so the card descriptions in *Tarot: Your Everyday Guide* are adapted accordingly. You interpret a card in terms of things that you can do, and the central figure in the card, which usually represents the querent, models what ought to be done.

This book is especially concerned with practical matters, applying the tarot's advice to common problems and situations that many people are concerned about, such as whether to say "yes" or "no" to an offer, whether or not to become involved in some cause or conflict, choosing between job and educational options, starting or ending relationships, and dealing with difficult people.

1-56718-565-7, 312 pp., 7½ x 9⅛ $12.95

Tarot Plain and Simple

Anthony Louis
with illustrations by
Robin Wood

The Tarot is an excellent method for turning experience into wisdom. At its essence the Tarot deals with archetypal symbols of the human situation.

By studying the Tarot, we connect ourselves with the mythical underpinnings of our lives; we contact the gods within. As a tool, the Tarot helps to awaken our intuitive self. This book presents a thoroughly tested, reliable, and user-friendly self-study program for those who want to do readings for themselves and others. It is written by a psychiatrist who brings a profound understanding of human nature and psychological conflict to the study of the Tarot. Tarot enthusiasts will find that his Jungian approach to the card descriptions will transport them to an even deeper level of personal transformation.

1-56718-400-6, 336 pp., 6 x 9, illus. $14.95

Tarot for Beginners
An Easy Guide to Understanding & Interpreting the Tarot

P. Scott Hollander

The Tarot is much more than a simple divining tool. While it can—and does—give you accurate and detailed answers to your questions when used for fortunetelling, it can also lead you down the road to self-discovery in a way that few other meditation tools can do. *Tarot for Beginners* will tell you how to use the cards for meditation and self-enlightenment as well as for divination.

If you're just beginning a study of the Tarot, this book gives you a basic, straightforward definition of the meaning of each card that can be easily applied to any system of interpretation, with any Tarot deck, using any card layout. The main difference between this book and other books on the Tarot is that it's written in plain English—you need no prior knowledge of the Tarot or other arcane subjects to understand its mysteries, because this no-nonsense guide will make the symbolism of the Tarot completely accessible to you. You will receive an overview of of the cards of the Major and Minor Arcana in terms of their origin, purpose, and interpretive uses as well as clear, in-depth descriptions and interpretations of each card.

1-56718-363-8, 352 pp., 5 ¼ x 8, illus. $12.95

Tarot Journeys
Adventures in Self-Transformation

Yasmine Galenorn
includes audio CD with
selected meditations
from the book

The Tarot has long been used for divination, but now you can use it to guide your growth and change. Tarot Journeys offers a complete guided meditation, or lyrical story, for each of the twenty-two cards of the Major Arcana, which will teach you more about each card than you thought possible. Come to understand the spiritual nature of the energy behind each archetype, as well as the ways in which it relates to the cycles of your life.

Like the journey of the Fool (the first card of the Major Arcana), *Tarot Journeys* will guide you through the major choices and cycles that face everyone—from choosing a life-path to love, from personal sacrifice to shoring up self-esteem, from coping with the material world to searching for inner spirit. The meditations flow like classic fables, leading you through exotic imaginary lands, and guiding you into unexpected encounters with mythical people and creatures.

1-56718-264-X, 288 pp., 7½ x 9⅛ $19.95

How to Read the Tarot
The Keyword System

Sylvia Abraham

In as little as one week's time you could be amazing your friends with the accuracy of your insights, when you study the easy-to-learn Keyword system of Tarot reading! Here is a simple and practical guide to interpreting the symbolic language of the Tarot that anyone can quickly learn to use with any Tarot deck.

Unlike other Tarot books that provide key word interpretations, *How to Read the Tarot* provides an interpretive structure that applies to the card numbers of both the Major and Minor Arcana. In the Keyword system, for example, every number "Two" card (the Two card of each suit in the Minor Arcana as well as The High Priestess, the Two card of the Major Arcana) has a basic "I KNOW" key phrase. These simple key phrases are then combined with the symbolic meaning of the four suits, to give you a rich source from which to draw your interpretations. The book includes five spreads and a dictionary of symbols.

Few Tarot books on the market are as concise and accessible as this one—and no other book shows how to use this unique system.

1-56718-001-9, 272 pp., mass market $4.99